At the Borders
of Sleep

At the Borders

Borders

ON LIMINAL LITERATURE

of Sleep

Peter Schwenger

University of Minnesota Press
Minneapolis
London

Published by the University of Minnesota Press
111 Third Avenue South, Suite 290
Minneapolis, MN 55401-2520
http://www.upress.umn.edu

Library of Congress Cataloging-in-Publication Data
Schwenger, Peter, 1942–
At the borders of sleep : on liminal literature / Peter Schwenger.
Includes bibliographical references and index.
ISBN 978-0-8166-7975-1 (hc : alk. paper)
ISBN 978-0-8166-7976-8 (pb : alk. paper)
1. Literature—History and criticism—Theory. 2. Liminality.
3. Consciousness. I. Title.
PN441.S385 2012
809'.933561—dc23   2012020152

Printed in the United States of America on acid-free paper

The University of Minnesota is an equal-opportunity educator and employer.

19 18 17 16 15 14 13 12   10 9 8 7 6 5 4 3 2 1

CONTENTS

PREFACE

"Sleep, perhaps, has never been philosophical," Jean-Luc Nancy once remarked.[1] Perhaps. For if philosophy has not managed to contain sleep within itself, neither has it quite managed to forget it. The problem of sleep is always hovering at the edges of rational thought, which has traditionally been identified with a state of clear-eyed wakefulness. Sleep, in contrast, is depicted as the sodden state of those who do not think. Yet those who do think find that sleep troubles their waking moments, as in Descartes's famous poser about whether you can be entirely sure that you are not at this moment only dreaming that you are awake.[2] Even to find words for what happens to us when we sleep is extraordinarily difficult, let alone the task of accounting philosophically for it. This study of the borders of sleep, then, begins at the borders of philosophy: we need to consider, if only briefly, the nature of this sleep that eludes philosophers—and also eludes this book. For though the word *sleep* appears in each of its sections, this will be a book not about sleep but about sleep's edges. This is so for reasons I must now explain, and first by returning to Jean-Luc Nancy.

In the pages that follow Nancy's observation, he teases out the implications of one significant exception to philosophy's neglect of sleep: a set of brief passages in Hegel's *Philosophy of Mind*. It is a curious treatment of the topic. On one hand, Hegel seems to subscribe to the accepted philosophical identification of waking with consciousness and rational thought, identifying sleep as the opposite of this.

On the other hand, it soon becomes evident that simply to gesture toward sleep as the opposite of the waking state is not sufficient, since the state of sleep demands that we understand it on its own terms, terms that are not those of our waking thought. Most of all, the problem arises of how these two states are linked, as they are at each day's beginning and end. The transition from sleep to waking soon becomes for Hegel a paradigm of the way that self-consciousness and self "itself" come into being.

If in Hegel's metaphysical version of sleep there is no self yet, what is it that is asleep? His term for that entity is "soul." Disentangling the soul from its common religious connotations, we must see it, in Nancy's words, as "the individual identity that has not acquired or conquered or produced its identity—and that will nevertheless *endure* throughout the whole process of the subject" ("Identity and Trembling" 17). A paradoxical formulation, this identity that is not yet a (self-produced) identity. It is essentially being defined as that which "endures" during a process; and the burden of defining this entity is shifted to defining the process. That process is the transition from sleep to waking, with all that Hegel makes depend upon it.

We initially find the soul, then, within sleep, from which it cannot be distinguished: "Sleep," Hegel says, "is the state in which the soul is immersed in its differenceless unity" (67). If differenceless, then the soul cannot be differentiated from sleep; its awakening is precisely a matter of differentiation, during which a soul becomes a self, conscious of its selfhood as distinguished from what is other than itself: "The waking state includes generally all self-conscious and rational activity in which the mind realizes its own distinct self" (65). While this process seems like an evolution, a privileging of the waking and rational state, Hegel's description of sleep immediately following this sentence is rather different from philosophy's traditional characterization:

> Sleep is an invigoration of this [self-conscious and rational] activity—not as a merely negative rest from it, but as a return back from the world of specialization, from dispersion into phases where it has grown hard and stiff—a return into the general nature of subjectivity, which is the substance of those specialized energies and their absolute master. (65)

Sleep, that is, is a "substance" that is not merely inert and stupefied but the primal source out of which any distinctions must be carved. To sleep is, in the words of Emmanuel Levinas, to withdraw "into the plenum" (70). To wake, then, is always to emerge into something less than everything. The "specialized energies" of consciousness are won through excluding large portions of "the general nature of subjectivity." So one's daily waking—as I shall be arguing later— can bring with it a subtle sense of melancholy as one reenters a diminished existence. This is a quotidian reenactment of what, according to Hegel, is involved in the primal process of becoming a self-conscious subject.

That process still remains elusive—in Hegel, and in Nancy's commentary on Hegel. "Waking," Hegel says, "is brought about by the lightning-stroke of subjectivity breaking through the form of the mind's immediacy" (67). While he of course says a good deal more than this, what does not, cannot, get explained is what exactly impels the motion of transition. Nancy too makes various attempts to describe the transition, of which this one may be representative: "The soul is awakening—but awakening, strictly speaking, is only the subject floating up to the surface of sleep, passing along the surface of sleep; or, again, it is only sleep itself taking the figure—barely figurable—of the subject" ("Identity and Trembling" 16). Both thinkers, faced with a transitional force that eludes them, must necessarily resort to metaphors at this point. "This point," it should be stressed, is a *liminal* one. We are trying to come to terms with a threshold between two states that are literally as different as day and night—and yet can change into each other and perhaps even interpenetrate.

I have ventured into these murky philosophical waters not to resolve the problems I have outlined but simply to give a sense of what is at stake in any consideration of the borders of sleep. Waking, drowsiness, insomnia (almost always more liminal than simple wide-awakeness)—these states will be the subject matter of this book. Subtle and elusive in themselves, they are also involved with some of philosophy's subtlest problems. And to the degree that philosophy's habitual tools are those of the waking world—distinction, selection, and logic deployed in unusually rigorous ways—those tools will inevitably fall short of the nocturnal mode. And that is why we are confined to the *borders* of sleep, rather than venturing into the darkness of sleep proper.

If sleep is a plenum, it is also an absence; and this is not as contradictory as it may sound. In sleep, true sleep stripped of consciousness, we become once more a thing. We are then reabsorbed into a world from which we were distanced by the act of observing it as a subject views an object. That object can be our own interior life, as Hegel makes clear: "We have defined sleep as the state in which the soul distinguishes itself *neither inwardly nor from the outer world*" (68–69; emphasis mine). Without distinctions of any kind, there can only be a plenum. But though we may arrive at this conclusion through logical thought, that is something very different from *knowing* the plenum; for knowing demands precisely the consciousness that is excluded by sleep. Sleep is an absence, then—the absence of a self, and of the consciousness that is needed for any knowledge of what is being experienced by whatever is experiencing it.

I need to stress here that to speak of sleep is not to speak of dream, though there is a common inclination to confuse the two, both within philosophy and without. Dream and sleep are not to be simply equated. Monitoring of the body's functions has established that dreaming occurs intermittently during the night, with the total amount of sleep time spent dreaming being about 25 percent. The same monitoring techniques have also led to a surprising conclusion about those periods when rapid eye movement coincides with other body signals to indicate that dreaming is taking place: "*Rapid eye movement sleep and wakefulness are fundamentally equivalent functional states*" (Llinas and Paré 522). Dreams, we are told by the same researchers, "can be considered as a modified attentive state in which attention is turned away from the sensory input, toward memories" (525). However, the brain's functioning is essentially the same in dreaming as it is in waking. So Maurice Blanchot can write, "Sleep grows sleepless in dreams" ("Dreaming, Writing" xxviii).[3] The dream is a sort of waking on the other bank of the Lethean river that is sleep. Of the version of waking that is the dream side of sleep I will be saying little: dreams have always received extraordinary amounts of attention. But not much attention has been paid to the other edge of sleep, the one in which our familiar waking consciousness meets the world of sleep, either coming or going. "Every Exit Is an Entrance" Anne Carson titles an essay, which has for its subtitle "A Praise of Sleep." And indeed at that threshold one really does not know, in the idiomatic sense of the phrase, whether one is coming or going. There is a confusion of the familiar waking perceptions that can be felt as such only because there is enough of a waking consciousness still present to know that here is something it does not know. Things are different on the far side of sleep, where one subscribes without question to the logic, or antilogic, of the dream world, only seeking to make sense of it later on, in the daylight. For this reason—that at the hither side of sleep one can watch the very transition from reason to something beyond reason—it has seemed worthwhile to investigate the various manifestations of this threshold or liminal state. For they are various, and sometimes enfold each other, transform into each other.

Each chapter of this book is devoted to one such liminal state. "Toward Sleep" deals with the onset of drowsiness and the alterations of perception that come with that; this includes the phenomenon of hypnagogia, the images that present themselves as if of their own accord before the closed eyes of a subject who is not yet asleep. "Sleepless" deals with insomnia, and what is at stake—philosophically and psychologically—in this involuntary encounter with the night. "Leaving Sleep" analyzes the transition of waking, the ways that we return from what can rightly be called an altered state of consciousness to our usual sense of a conscious self—though not perhaps without a significant residue. Finally, "Sleepwaking" takes a step back to consider the implications of the preceding chapters, but taken all together to postulate an inescapable liminality.

These investigations are carried out primarily through literature. I have used philosophy, and at times science, to help my thinking; but only literature, I would contend, has the subtlety to deal with such liminal sensations. If literature's insights are not conveyed in the form of a coherent philosophical argument or system, that may be as much a virtue as a vice. Since liminal moments are marked by a dissipation of coherence as one state dissolves into another, to render them in systematic terms is to distort them, and finally to lose them altogether. Even rigorous philosophers such as Nancy and Hegel, as we have seen, resort to literary means such as metaphor to convey something that can be apprehended only indirectly. But it *can* be apprehended, if not contained or finally defined. The sense of a system is often diffused throughout a literary text; and this may convey an understanding that is more meaningful than an abstract argument: as John Keats observed, "Axioms in philosophy are not axioms until they are proved upon our pulses" (letter to J. H. Reynolds, May 3, 1818).

While literature is here the means of understanding liminal states, the reverse is also true: liminal states throughout are used to speak of the ways in which literature is itself a liminal state, for both the writer and the reader. The "liminal literature" of my subtitle, then, is not just a certain body of writing that deals with states at the threshold of sleep—though it is that, of course. It is also literature in general, considered under its liminal aspects. If, as Jorge Luis Borges has asserted, literature is nothing more than a guided dream (20), the dream aspect is arrived at through a state of uncommon alertness to the implications of the words on the page. While reading, the mind moves in many directions simultaneously: remembering the text already read, anticipating the text to come, plumbing the implications of what is beneath the reader's eye at the moment. At the same time, as I will be arguing in the section titled "The Obbligato Effect," the mind is moving within itself to produce a rich flickering of associations and images. These arise not directly from the text but from a realm—notoriously difficult to define—that is more akin to dream than to waking processes of meaning making. To characterize the reading of a literary text as either a fully conscious and rational activity *or* an immersion into dream is at either extreme to distort the experience. Literature is liminal; and this is so for both the reader and the writer.

Here it might be objected that there is in fact no experience that is not liminal, poised between what it has been and what it is in the process of becoming. Nancy indeed makes a similar argument in *The Fall of Sleep*, evolving it somewhat unexpectedly out of the analysis of a rocking cradle:

Rocking movements put us to sleep because sleep in its essence is itself a rocking, not a stable, motionless state. [Rocking is a matter] of the initial beat between something and nothing, between the world and the void, which also means between the world and itself.

It is a matter of the space in between, without which no reality can take place and without which, accordingly, no reality is real without a connection to some other reality from which it is separated by the interval that distinguishes them and that links them to each other according to the very pulsation of their common nonorigin *[in-origine]*—since in fact nothing makes or marks origin, nothing but the spacing and balancing of *nihil* among things, beings, substances or subjects, positions, places, times. Nothing but the swaying of the world makes the cradle or rather cradling within which everything wakens—awakening to sleep as well as to waking. (30–31)

The "space in between" is a liminal one, and Nancy's sweeping assertion once more underscores the importance of these liminal states between waking and sleep. Liminality is not a weird exception to the normal state of existence; it *is* that state. These states at the borders of sleep are simply more dramatic ways of reminding us of that.

This preface is of course also liminal, almost by definition if not by etymology. Derrida has analyzed the ways in which a preface is never *pre-*. Pretending to precede another text, it is a supplement to what must in fact already be there. This preface, too, has been the last part of the book to be written; so for me it is something of an exit. For you, the reader, however, it is an entrance, a threshold, a transition from your usual ways of thinking into other possible ways of thinking. Whether those ways partake of waking or dreaming or (as I would hope) both, it must now be up to you to decide.

ONE

Toward Sleep

In a passing observation, Maurice Merleau-Ponty compares sleep to a god—which indeed for the ancient Greeks it was. As a god, sleep may be as fickle as any other, giving or withholding its favors at will. At one time it possesses us without our consent; at another it refuses to be courted, supplicated even. We know of only one way to invoke the god, and that is to imitate him so faithfully that we are merged with his being. Here is the passage, from *Phenomenology of Perception*:

> As the faithful, in the Dionysian mysteries, invoke the god by mim-
> ing scenes from his life, I call up the visitation of sleep by imitating
> the breathing and posture of the sleeper. . . . There is a moment
> when sleep "comes," settling on this imitation of itself which I have
> been offering to it, and I succeed in becoming what I was trying
> to be: an unseeing and almost unthinking mass, riveted to a point
> in space and in the world henceforth only through the anonymous
> alertness of the senses. (163–64)

These alert senses are "half-open doors," Merleau-Ponty says, through which the sleeper, waking, may return to the world. How "anonymous" the senses are in sleep may of course be disputed. Some glimmering of one's particular consciousness remains; it weighs and interprets the sensory stimulus. The faint and distant cry of a baby may wake a parent who will sleep through much louder noises, if these are registered as habitual or harmless.

As for "the moment when sleep 'comes,'" it is no wonder that Merleau-Ponty puts this arrival in quotation marks. There is something in it of the same paradox that Maurice Blanchot has famously asserted of death (Thantos, the twin brother of Hypnos): that we can never know death because the instant of death is also the instantaneous end of knowing. Similarly, the actual moment when sleep comes must always elude us. Though we may be aware of sleep's preliminary signs (a lethargy of the limbs, a loosening of our associative processes), the moment when we slip over the border into sleep is also the one in which we lose awareness—at least awareness in its usual versions. William James once compared the introspective analysis of consciousness to "trying to turn up the gas quickly enough to see how the darkness looks" (1:244). The same difficulty applies in analyzing the transition to unconsciousness that is the onset of sleep.

The futility of trying to pinpoint the moment that sleep arrives is demonstrated at length in a passage from Danilo Kiš's novel *Garden, Ashes*:

> I let myself be lulled, I even tried with all my strength to lull myself to sleep, and then I would jerk my head at the last moment, when I thought I was catching myself *sinking into sleep*. But I was never wholly satisfied with this torturous experiment. Sometimes I woke up ten times in a row, with the last effort of my consciousness. . . . But it always seemed to me to be not the right moment, it seemed that I had made rash moves, because I never succeeded in getting so much as a peek into sleep, and my intention had been exactly that. Instead, once I had roused myself before the very gates of sleep, the angel [of sleep] would have taken flight, would have hidden somewhere behind my head, in some mousehole, who knows where. On one occasion, though, I seemed to have caught sleep in the act, *in flagrante delicto* as it were. I was saying to myself, thinking to myself:

"I am awake, I am awake." I lay there waiting with this thought as though in an ambush, waiting for someone—the angel of sleep or God—to dispute my thought, to come and deny my thought and prevent me from thinking it. I would have wanted to verify who the angel of sleep was and how it was capable of halting all at once the flow of my thoughts—this one simple sentence, to be exact, this bare thought that I did not want to surrender without a struggle. At that point, tormented by the strain of avoiding the surrender of this thought, and in the absence of the angel of sleep (who failed to come to dispute me and must have been aware of the fact that I was observing), I resorted to a trick: I would cease to think that thought so as to make the angel believe that I had decided, incautious and overcome by fatigue, to surrender without resistance, to close my eyes. Yet it was not easy to stop thinking this simple thought of mine—"I am awake"—all at once, for this thought had broken off on its own, carried along by inertia. The harder I tried not to think it, the more obtrusive it became, just as when I tried not to hear the ticking of the alarm clock on the nightstand I became more clearly aware of its tick-tock, tick-tock than ever. And when I finally succeeded in forgetting this thought, really and truly, I would sink into sleep without knowing how it had happened, just as I succeeded in not hearing the ticking of the clock only when I was not thinking about it or when I was already asleep. Nonetheless, as I was saying, I actually succeeded in rousing myself at precisely the moment when the wings had covered my eyes like a shadow and when I was suddenly struck by some intoxicating whiff: I had awakened from real sleep at the instant when the angel of sleep had come to take me away, yet I saw nothing, found out nothing. I finally understood that the presence of my consciousness and the presence of the angel of sleep were mutually exclusive, but I continued playing this tiring and dangerous game for a long time. (18–20)[1]

Kiš's narrator is here playing a thought game, a game with thoughts. His assumption is that sleep is "capable of halting all at once the flow of my thoughts." It is more accurate, however, to say that sleep comes *by means of* the flow of one's thoughts, a flow that becomes a drift. What Kiš's narrator calls "this simple thought of mine" is neither simple nor a thought; it is a sentence: "I am awake." A sentence, we have been told repeatedly, expresses a complete thought; but in any sentence there is an excess, something leading to the sentence and anticipating certain possible movements out of it, not to speak (yet) of the multiple resonances that accompany it. William James again: "We name our thoughts simply, each after its thing, as if each knew its own thing and nothing else. What each really knows is clearly the thing it is named for, with dimly perhaps a thousand other things. It ought to be named after all of them, but it never is. . . . Every definite image in the mind is steeped and dyed in the free water that flows round it" (1:241, 255). It is this "free water" of consciousness that sweeps in like a tide, bringing sleep with it. Any attempt to hold on to the daylight comprehension of a sentence while entering into the night can only deteriorate into repetition—a repetition that itself contributes to the emptying out of meaning, until what is left is a mere shell, as mechanical as the ticking of the clock to which it is here compared. Meanwhile, something else is going on as sleep "comes," something very different from the play with sleep as a kind of on/off switch.

Aris Fioretos, attempting to capture something of what is involved with the onset of sleep, describes in *The Gray Book* an altogether more gradual process. He first gives a detailed description of the variations in blackness, or grayness, that can be distinguished by the eye within the closed eyelids. And then:

> The more we focus on this downy density, the more we notice how it moves, glides, or rather floats, and after a while we are convinced that whatever it is, it is not exactly solid, but consists of innumerable layers closely compressed and folded. . . . Soft arrays of cloudiness, weighted with languor and abandon. After sinking for a while, we realize we are in the process of falling asleep and that the thick thud with which vapor is wrapping us must be sleep itself that has arrived. Finally. Yet . . . Wait. Hold it. Just this: in order to be embraced by such feathery fold, descending like slow tender fog, it is not enough to be ready, tucked away like a knife under a pillow, but an action is required that, however, demands passiveness more than activity, and while it appears to be simplicity itself, we believe it will prove exacting. Not only does it require us to reduce the body to a point without extension, like an empty pupil contracting nil but not being null, at the same time it turns the two-dimensional space

in front of us into a vaulted enclosure. . . . And while we are falling, and falling waiting for the moment when we shall pass over the
threshold without being aware of it, finally embraced by amity and
placidness, we begin to make out the images hovovering [sic] around
us. (2–3)

Fioretos's prose is overwrought, to be sure, but not inappropriate to
a state in which the moorings to conventional structure and perception are in the process of being cast off. In their place emerge those
"images," images that belong precisely to the transitional state when
one is slipping over into sleep. These are the images of *hypnagogia*.

WRITING HYPNAGOGIA

Here is a fairly representative description of the way hypnagogia
progresses. You are in bed, your eyes are closed, you feel yourself
slipping toward sleep. Drowsily you become aware of bright clouds
drifting past, which condense into floating luminous ribbons, stars,
saw-toothed lines, and geometrical forms. Then the faces begin: they
crowd in on you, grotesque to the point of caricature. One group
pares itself down to skulls, and it is now clear that they are a skel-
eton family, rather jolly, mother and father and two children with
balloons, all seated in a bulbous automobile, and moving along in the
jerky fashion of 1930s cartoons. They disappear down a long curving
road, which then unfolds like a wave . . . .[2]

As the word's etymology indicates, hypnagogia leads into sleep,
which is why many people are unaware of experiencing it. While
hypnagogic images usually end up turning into dream images, we
can, and should, distinguish between them. The difference is immediately apparent on those occasions when one finds that particular
notch where hypnagogia displays its powers. In the hypnagogic state,
observation is from a distance: the images appear as if projected upon
a screen, and one is oddly detached, observing the phenomenon with
interest and curiosity. This is the part of us that is awake, so much
so that people in this state can perform simple tasks or carry on conversations about what they are seeing, with full consciousness of its
illusory nature (Mavromatis 28). Dreams, in contrast, wholly enfold

us within their world; only at intervals do we manage to remind ourselves that this is, that this has to be, a dream.

Where do these hypnagogic images come from? In the mid-nineteenth century, Alfred Maury suggested that they are produced by entoptic stimuli—that is, by stimuli occurring within the eyeball rather than originating from without. These have various causes, the most common being imperfections in the fluid of the eye and floating cell debris. To the observer, they may appear as pulsations of light and drifting filaments that can be "seen" in darkness or with closed eyes. Maury's explanation has been sustained through a long line of thinkers such as Bergson, Freud, and Havelock Ellis; it has allowed them to move quickly past this presleep phenomenon into consideration of the world of dreams. Too quickly. For there are aspects of hypnagogic imagery that can scarcely be accounted for by Maury's explanation. Foremost among these is the extreme specificity and focus of hypnagogic imagery, a "heightened reality" (Mavromatis 30), which cannot be readily explained as the mental elaboration of vague stimuli within the eye. Mental images are never this clear, this perceptually present; indeed, one informant was able to create mental images even as the more vivid hypnagogic images continued to unroll before him (Mavromatis 28).

It was perhaps peculiarities such as these that led Jean-Paul Sartre, while surveying the modes of image in his *Psychology of Imagination,* to spend more time on hypnagogia than on any other mode. His analysis is a curious combination of blindness and insight. While accepting the theory of entoptic stimuli as the basis for hypnagogic images, he investigates, far more fully than his predecessors, the ways in which those stimuli are transformed. For entoptic stimuli do not actually have the characteristic shapes of early hypnagogia, such as saw-toothed lines, stars, or geometrical forms; rather, "in apprehending them, they are apprehended *as* teeth of a saw or *as* stars" (65). That is, a phenomenological intentionality is at work here—to such an extraordinary degree that Sartre invokes a certain "fatality," as he calls it, in contrast to determinism. The difference is that while determinism is a series of steps leading toward an event that is the inevitable outcome of those steps, "fatalism posits that such an event should happen and that it is this coming event that determines the series that is to lead up to it" (67). But this is surely to negate the initial and deterministic role of entoptic stimuli, replacing it with a "coming event" that arises from the dynamic of apprehension; and this now requires an explanation of its own. The best that Sartre can do is to gesture toward the mental faculty that sees a face in a blot or a flame or a wallpaper pattern; however, this intentionality is "free and aware of its spontaneity" (60) in a way that hypnagogia is not.

Nor, when we see a face in the fire, does it go on to reveal itself as, say, one of a series of marble statues adorning a piece of imposing architecture, which then metamorphoses in its turn. Hypnagogic imagery, in contrast to our fireside fantasy, continually and rapidly changes. Sartre offers a number of explanations for this fact, which are not entirely convincing:

1. "The very course of chained thought which is never short of inter-pretation." "Chained" here means both linked and bound, as in association, which is never "free"; but if this is true of associative thought, it does not account for the leap to distinct perception.

2. "Changes in the entoptic field." This works only if we accept the causal function of entoptic phenomena, which falls short of a full accounting.

3. "The movement of the eyeballs." But Sartre has earlier suggested that in the hypnagogic state the eyeballs are fixed in a kind of paralysis by autosuggestion, receiving the image passively, in con-trast to the rapid eye movements that accompany dreaming. This is the state that Sartre calls *fascination* (68).

Blanchot employs the term *fascination* as well in "The Two Ver-sions of the Imaginary," where he uses it to describe the dark side, as it were, of our relationship to image. In contrast to the project of control over things that images often serve, "the undetermined milieu of fascination" takes us into a realm where "the image is pas-sivity, where it has no value either significative or affective, but is the passion of indifference" (*Space* 263). Here as elsewhere in his essay Blanchot might well be describing the experience of hypnagogia.

Neither perception nor representation, each of which is linked to things in the world, hypnagogia is no more adequately accounted for as "mental images," from which it is distinguished by the extraordinary clarity of what is sensed as appearing before the eyes. Hallucination, that state in which a subjective image is experienced as an external reality, might be a more adequate category—except that in hypnagogia the real, as Blanchot puts it, enters an "equivocal realm" (262), one in which the images are viewed as real enough, but not so real that one imagines any kind of concrete reality behind them. Sartre admits this paradox: "I really do see something, but what I see *is nothing*. This is the reason why this chained consciousness takes the form of an *image*: because it does not reach its own end" (70). Sartre's language at the end of this comment is in accord with Blanchot's description of what it means "to live an event as an image":

> It is to be taken: to pass from the region of the real where we hold ourselves at a distance from things the better to order and use them into that other region where the distance holds us—the distance which then is the lifeless deep, an unmanageable, inappreciable remoteness which has become something like the sovereign power behind all things. This movement implies infinite degrees. (*Space* 261)

Hypnagogic vision conforms uncannily to this description. It enacts a dynamic of pure image, a dynamic that not only detaches the image from any material reality but also fails to reattach it to anything else. The subject is plunged, metaphysically, into an interminable movement, one that is physically expressed by the continuously changing nature of hypnagogic imagery.

All this makes of hypnagogia a fundamental challenge to literature. A. Alvarez, for one, has stated that hypnagogic images are "unmediated by language and wholly impervious to art, narrative and interpretation." They lie "outside the range of literature" because of their intensely visual character and the speed at which the images change (152). Nevertheless, some writers, as different as Nathaniel Hawthorne and Christa Wolf,[3] have been prompted by specific hypnagogic images. And a single hypnagogic experience is credited by André Breton with providing the genesis of the entire surrealist movement.[4] Edgar Allan Poe saw the relation between the writer and hypnagogic images as a consummation devoutly to be wished, but unlikely to be attained. In an essay for *Graham's Magazine* on the powers and limits of writing, he speaks of a class of "fancies" that arise "where the confines of the waking world blend with those of the world of dreams" (258, 259). In his investigations, Poe asserts, he has reached the point of being able first to evoke these fancies at will and then to prevent the transition to sleep that so easily follows. Enabled in this way to survey this phenomenon "with the eye of analysis," he concludes cautiously, "I do not altogether despair of embodying in words at least enough of the fancies in question to convey to certain classes of intellect, a shadowy conception of their character" (259).

We may ask, then, to what degree Poe's hopes have been realized in literature. What techniques have been used in an attempt to do justice to—or at least provide "a shadowy conception of"— hypnagogic phenomena? What implications are conveyed by literary treatments of these phenomena? And finally, what insights into the experience of literature itself can we gain by considering its relation to the hypnagogic state? I will approach these questions in the same order I have posed them: first limiting the literature I look at to works that clearly attempt to reproduce something of the hypnagogic effect; then moving to works that are less clearly about hypnagogia; and finally returning to the large question that Alvarez poses about the range and nature of literature.

The best-known work about hypnagogia (though seldom recognized as such)[5] is Robert Frost's "After Apple-Picking." Whatever else this richly resonant poem may be about, it is rooted in a specific kind of hypnagogic experience, the perseverative: repetition before one's closed eyes of a visual stimulus that has been repeatedly enacted during the day (Mavromatis 48–49). So, as the poem's speaker is "drowsing off,"

> Magnified apples appear and disappear,
> Stem end and blossom end,
> And every fleck of russet showing clear.

The excess of the day's labors is carrying over into the night's. And the speaker, to use Blake's terms, has had enough, or rather too much:

"too much / Of apple-picking"—and indeed of all the striving of human life, for which this one labor can stand. Thus, as sleep overtakes the speaker, he is unsure of its real nature. Whether it is "just some human sleep," or death, or something else altogether, it will carry further what Mavromatis argues is "the core psychological phenomenon out of which springs the whole gamut of hypnagogic experiences . . . the loosening of the ego boundaries of the subject" (12).

This loosening of ego boundaries entails a loosening of control. In the case of hypnagogic images they can on occasion be controlled, changed, by their viewer (Mavromatis 71–77). Generally, however, they change according to a logic of their own, one that is not always congenial to the perceiver. So Richard Wilbur's "Walking to Sleep," a long poem about hypnagogic imagery couched as a set of useful tips, begins by urging confidence—

> Step off assuredly into the blank of your mind.
> Something will come to you.

—but then immediately undermines itself with a series of warnings:

> Try to remember this: what you project
> Is what you will perceive; what you perceive
> With any passion, be it love or terror,
> May take on whims and powers of its own.
> Therefore a numb and grudging circumspection
> Will serve you best, unless you overdo it . . . .

The poem continues by describing the perils of overdoing it, which could be corrected by measures that have perils of their own, and so on. There is no stability in this realm, neither in the sense of a consistently adequate strategy of control nor in any cessation of the relentlessly metamorphosing images. The hypnagogic traveler can only, in a steady pentameter,

> pursue an ever-dimming course
> Of pure transition, treading as in water
> Past crumbling tufa, down cloacal halls
> Of boarded-up hotels, through attics full

Of glassy taxidermy, moping on
Like a drugged fire-inspector.

"Pure transition" returns us to Blanchot's notion of image. For image, detached from material substance, partakes of the interminable nature of dream, which continually recedes from any postulated center. "The dream is the reawakening of the interminable," Blanchot writes (*Space* 267)—thus an awakening within the immobile body of sleep into a branching mobility of associations.

While hypnagogia is not dream, it has many of the visual qualities of dream. These, according to Lacan, overturn what is usually elided in our waking state: the realization that the image is not something that we look at from a detached position of control, but rather something that *shows* itself. "In the field of dream," he says, "what characterizes the images is that *it shows*" (*Four Fundamental Concepts* 75).[6] Significantly ungrammatical, this sentence's point is not merely that *they*—the images—show, but that through them *it* shows. This "it" is perhaps the "Es" of Freud's formulation *Wo Es war, soll Ich werden*—or of Blanchot's reformulation of it, *Là où je rêve, cela veille*: "Where I dream, it is awake" ("Dreaming, Writing" xxvii). In both dream and the predream state of hypnagogia, "I" gives way to "it," and does so through an autonomy of images. So Lacan can assert that "our position in the dream is profoundly that of someone who does not see. The subject does not see where it is leading, he follows" (75). The fascinated subject has given up control to that which shows itself before him, the images that arise from an "it" that is richly, profoundly other. In the case of hypnagogic images, indeed, the images defy any classic dream analysis: they hardly ever arise from "the day's residues" (except in the case of the perseverative type), nor do they yield any insight about the psyche of the person who perceives them; rather, they seem to arise from something other than a personal unconscious.

This disconcerting fecundity is reflected in the structure of Wilbur's poem: it continually promises to control and contain its images, but whenever it seems to be arriving at a resting point the poem unfolds into yet more imagery, taking shape, or rather shapelessness, as one long verse paragraph until it reaches a conclusion—which turns out to be delusory. Wilbur tells us what the hypnagogic traveler hopes for:

> that at some point of the pointless journey,
> Indoors or out, and when you least expect it,
> Right in the middle of your stride, like that,
> So neatly that you never feel a thing,
> The kind assassin Sleep will draw a bead
> And blow your brains out.

After all the preliminary hovering clauses, there could not be a more definitive period. But after a space, the only one in the poem, the half line is completed with

> What, are you still awake?

and the hypnagogic journey, with the stream of advice that accompanies it, starts all over again. It ends only with another version of the hope for sleep, significantly less final than the first one:

> if you are in luck, you may be granted,
> As, inland, one can sometimes smell the sea,
> A moment's perfect carelessness, in which
> To stumble a few steps and sink to sleep
> In the same clearing where, in the old story,
> A holy man discovered Vishnu sleeping,
> Wrapped in his maya, dreaming by a pool
> On whose calm face all images whatever
> Lay clear, unfathomed, taken as they came.

To take the images as they come, as they continually come, is the only advice that can be given in the end, in this end that is never ending. The stream of images—"all images whatever"—is inexhaustible. And each image, insofar as it *is* image, must necessarily be "unfathomed," for all its apparent limpidity.

Beyond Wilbur's poem about hypnagogia, this description may be applied to the imagery of any poem, to the degree that it eludes translation into an intellectual–allegorical equivalent. As it plays itself out in the reader's mind, imagery performs a kind of visual obbligato to the poem's narrative or argumentative line. It produces, we can say, an artificially induced hypnagogia that takes place with eyes wide open, one that is not the least important source of the poem's affect and consequent effect. The importance of this aspect varies, of course, with individual cases. A poet like John Ashbery, for instance, would seem to have moved hypnagogia from the boundary zone to the center of his work. He has said that "I tend to start with a few words and phrases that occur to me and that I have copied down on bits of paper, especially when falling asleep, or when I wake up in the morning" (Lopes interview 32).

If these phrases are hypnagogic, they are auditory rather than visual. For here we must recall that hypnagogia does not always confine itself to images. There are less common manifestations through other senses (Mavromatis 33–36), manifestations that we can find in "After Apple-Picking" alongside the visual ones: tactile ("My instep arch not only keeps the ache, / It keeps the pressure of a ladder-round") and auditory ("the rumbling sound / Of load on load of apples coming in"). Such manifestations are not common: they would seem to occur in about the same proportion as they occur within the predominant visuality of dream. However, when we are concerned with literature's relation to hypnagogia, the auditory form takes on a significance that is out of proportion to its statistical occurrence. Words, we realize, may not only be used to describe the hypnagogic phenomenon; they may at times *be* that phenomenon. Indeed, at times the sentences of auditory hypnagogia do sound rather like Ashbery's combination of syntactical verve and tilted sense. We get hypnagogic sentences such as "Buy stakes in the fixed stars. It is remarkably stable" or "Put the pink pyjamas in the salad" (Mavromatis 34, 38). As for Ashbery, "I hear voices," he has said, without explaining further (Koethe interview 184). Of course those voices may simply be fragments of conversation overheard in the street, which Ashbery also cites as a possible starting point for poetry. But only a starting point: whatever the sources of such phrases, they are just "a sort of gimmick to get started. Then one word seems to lead to another, and pretty soon I'm in the middle of writing a poem" (Lopes interview 32). Once the writing has taken shape,

Ashbery usually cuts out the phrases that were the poem's original impetus but now, he says, "stick out like sore thumbs. . . . It's almost like some sort of lost wax or other process where the initial armature gets scrapped in the end" (Bloom and Losada interview 14).

We cannot simply claim, then, that Ashbery has a hypnagogic muse and takes dictation from her. What does seem to be the case, though, is that he works within an aesthetic that goes beyond the realms of thought or perception as we generally allow ourselves to know them. Instead his poems open up to an associative play that is characteristic both of hypnagogia and of consciousness as Ashbery understands it—consciousness rather than the unconscious with which his poetry is often associated: "I would say that my poetry is really consciously trying to explore consciousness more than unconsciousness, although with elements of the unconscious to give it perspective" (Bloom and Losada interview 19). Shortly after, in the same interview, he says, "Every moment is surrounded by a lot of things in life that don't add up to anything that makes much sense and these are part of a situation that I feel I'm trying to deal with when I'm writing" (19). This focus on what is "surrounding" rather than what is front and center, on what is "in the shadows" rather than what is illuminated by the mind's eye—this indicates a poetry that is penumbral, but not exclusively so. The poems situate themselves in "the chamber behind the thought" ("Tone Poem" 112) but without the dissolution of thought. "On the whole," Ashbery has said, "I feel that poetry is going on all the time inside, an underground stream" (Stitt interview 405). This underground stream he brings to the surface of the page. Consciousness as he depicts it therefore replicates the obbligato effect that I have suggested is an important aspect of poetry very different from Ashbery's.

Among the literary genres, poetry is perhaps the one best suited to capture the hypnagogic phenomenon, since it so often aims at expressing subtle and evanescent states of mind. The novel, viewed as a sustained and structured narrative, is another matter altogether—but it need not for that reason be written out of the notion of a hypnagogic writing. Among authors a happy few incorporate a hypnagogic component within their novels, and thus stretch the boundaries of a genre that is almost defined by its continual experimentation.[7] Such are Giorgio de Chirico, James Joyce, and Alex Garland.

Giorgio de Chirico's *Hebdomeros* is a good candidate for the strangest novel ever written. It has no plot; in a sense it doesn't even have episodes. Its first sentence is a mysterious in medias res: " . . . And then began the visit to that strange building located in an austerely respectable but by no means dismal street." The eponymous hero and his friends carry revolvers in their pockets when they enter the building, a building that has "a history of being haunted by apparitions." Neither of these suspenseful elements is picked up. Instead, "Here we are!" says Hebdomeros, as they enter a large salon, in one corner of which "two gladiators wearing diving helmets were practicing halfheartedly" (3). This odd transition is compounded shortly after by a whole series of embedded associations, one within the other like multiple parentheses, which never return to the main line of the plot—if indeed such a thing exists. For example: "The broken vase was very valuable" (6). This is given to us as an example—though of what we are never sure—and is followed by the description of a family staring at a vase's fragments on the floor. "But," we are then told,

> no one ever went into the adjoining room. Here was the place of the buffet, the silver teapot and the dread of the great black cockroaches in the depths of the empty pots. It had never occurred to Hebdomeros to associate the idea of cockroaches and the idea of fish, but the two words *great* and *black* reminded him of a poignant scene, half-Homeric, half-Byronic, which he had once briefly witnessed toward evening on the rocky shores of an arid island. (7)

This sample may be enough to convey something of de Chirico's technique: the calm elegance of his writing masks the radical nature of the novel's continual shifts; so that *locally* what one is reading seems always to make sense, or at least to be about to make sense.

This illusion of logic is of course a characteristic of dreams. Why, then, am I not approaching *Hebdomeros* as a dream novel, rather than linking it to hypnagogia? It is true that the pace of the novel's transitions varies: at times a more sustained narrative element emerges, and these moments may seem more dreamlike than hypnagogic. However, as Mavromatis has observed, the pace of hypnagogic visions also varies. Hypnagogia, which often leads directly into sleep and dreams, may itself include dreamlike content, or at least visions that carry with them the *sensation* of narrative significance. A full description of that narrative significance may become indistinguishable from an actual narrative. If, as the truism has it, "a picture is worth a thousand words," it also *requires* a thousand words to evoke what the hypnagogic eye sees in an instant. The resulting slowdown may change the vision's basic experiential mode. Yet if certain scenes in *Hebdomeros* would require many sentences to be depicted adequately, at other points a single sentence can flicker with multiple shifts. For instance: "Where are you bound for, you of the coat with the astrakhan collar? You who are the prototype of the eternal traveler, always ready to protect the sick child from the grasping hands of bandits on this train that stinks of cattle soaked by an August downpour" (48).

Linking this sort of thing to hypnagogia is encouraged by some specific references in the text. The foot of Hebdomeros's bed is engraved with an image of "Mercury *oneiropompe,* that is, the bringer of dreams" (72). At the head of his bed is hung a painting that depicts "Mercury as a shepherd, holding a crook in place of his staff; he was driving before him toward the darkness of sleep his flock of dreams" (73). The movement *"toward* the darkness of sleep" while not yet being asleep is precisely that of hypnagogia. Another peculiar detail in the text makes more sense if it is read as an allusion to hypnagogic visions, which, we recall, are projected upon closed eyelids:

> The prefect worked in a cool room looking out onto a garden. The windows were open and the blinds lowered. Hebdomeros loved those blinds; sometimes, finding himself at the prefect's house, he would spend whole half-hours looking at them and lose himself in dreams before them, seeing there a peaceful countryside full of tranquil poetry. . . . (91)

What follows is a list of various other things seen there, which I omit. Shortly after, as Hebdomeros lies in his bed, he sees the classic patternings of the first stages of hypnagogia:

Charming ribbons, flames without heat darting like greedy tongues, disturbing bubbles, lines drawn with a brilliance even the memory of which he had thought long lost, soft waves, persistent and unvarying, rose and rose incessantly toward the ceiling of his room. (93)

The repetitive patterns and continual transformations of this passage are described in terms of *waves,* an image that occurs at regular intervals throughout the novel and is used to bring it to its close. At the novel's end, Hebdomeros has "opened wide his window" and at the same time "turned over on his couch" (115). In this state between dream and waking he asks, "What can I hope for now? In what still believe?" To this question he gets two answers, which are perhaps the same answer in two different modes. There is first an allegorical female, described by Hebdomeros as "thou whom I glimpse before my afternoon sleep; thou, visible to myself alone, thou whose glance speaks to me of immortality!" (116). And second, "a great wave, heavy and irresistible, of an infinite tenderness, had submerged everything [in a] new Ocean" (116). This ocean in turn separates into smaller waves that enact a distinctly hypnagogic transformation:

Waves whose yellow-green depths were wholly embroidered on the surface with foam broke inside out and great masses of wild mares, hoofs hard as steel, disappeared in an unbridled gallop, in an avalanche of rumps rubbing together, colliding, pushing toward infinity. (116)

Shortly after this, Hebdomeros, who has been pondering on what the visionary woman has given him to understand, abandons his thoughts completely: "They surrendered to the caressing waves of unforgettable words, and on these waves they floated toward strange and unknown shores" (117). These waves that are now words evoke the very novel we are just finishing. The sentence is a description of the threshold state to which the reader is expected to yield, without, as Keats has put it, "any irritable reaching after fact and reason." At the same time the suspended "toward" in this sentence echoes the earlier description of the waves "pushing toward infinity," an infinity that is the source of endless and inexhaustible images; in its way this too speaks of immortality. Finally, de Chirico's long run-on sentences might also be seen as wavelike—especially when they follow one another to make up paragraphs that go on for as long as nine pages, offering nothing in the way of a horizon by which to steer. The style in this way alludes to the continual transformations of hypnagogia.

The content of de Chirico's style is almost always visual, understandably so for a painter. The case is rather different with James Joyce, who once declared, "Painting does not interest me"(Ellmann 505). Yet hypnagogia—a primarily visual phenomenon—has been linked to *Finnegans Wake,* notably by Jeremy Lane. His adventurous essay "Falling Asleep in the *Wake*: Reading as Hypnagogic Experience" takes as a starting point John Bishop's emphasis on the degree to which Joyce was trying to write a book of the night, one reflecting our experiences when asleep—and then pushes this further. Lane quotes Joyce's words to Max Eastman: "In writing of the night, I really could not, I felt I could not, use words in their ordinary connections. Used that way they do not express how things are in the night, in the different stages—conscious, then semi-conscious, then unconscious" (163). Reading the *Wake,* Lane argues, we partake of an experience that is certainly not unconscious, since the book demands a more than usual degree of alertness and wakefulness; nor are we fully conscious, since we are absorbed in the disorientations of Joyce's night world. While reading this book we are then "semiconscious"—in a threshold state, which the flickering play of language suggests may be hypnagogic. Yet this effect is not achieved through a visual plethora evoked by words but by the words themselves, with their unstable tendency to puns and multiple meanings.

Words in Joyce's book are always overdetermined, signifying on many levels, even many languages, simultaneously. So in the following sentences Joyce might be referring to his own elusive book:

> Will whatever will be written in lappish language with inbursts of Maggyer always seem semposed, black looking white and white guarding black, in that siamixed twoatalk used twist stern swift and jolly roger? Will it bright upon us, nightle, and we plunging to our plight? (66)

The language described here is not merely a mixture of Lappish and

Magyar (or Hungarian): it is a "siamixed" twin that fuses words. Lappish language is also *lapsus linguae,* a slip of the tongue, for words in the *Wake* are constantly slipping away into other words and their associations. The extreme instability of the words makes it seem that the black and white of the written page change places, as do day and night. Thus the experience of Joyce's novel at a certain point will "bright upon us" in a traditional illumination at the same time that it will "nightle." That is, it will slide us on an iridescent slick of words toward an unconscious that is, as Lacan asserts, structured as a language—so "plunging [us] to our plight." Yet this is only a movement *toward,* one that does not thereby annihilate the daylight world. The letter's agency does its work neither wholly in consciousness nor in the unconscious.

Joyce's writing walks the line between the white and the black worlds, between words as we know them (or think we know them) and their dream distortions. Any reading of *Finnegans Wake* consequently takes place at a threshold zone. Perhaps, though, this is only an extreme version of what always happens when reading a novel: however straight the lines on the page, however straightforward the sentences may seem, the reader's unconscious darts in and out and between the words, evoking associations just barely beyond conscious awareness, but no less powerful for that. This is, in Lane's phrase, "reading as hypnagogic experience"—not only in the extreme case of *Finnegans Wake* but also to various degrees in any act of reading.[8]

All this implies a role for hypnagogia that is not necessarily confined to that certain notch between waking and sleeping. There are other conditions under which it may manifest itself, and which suggest that hypnagogia does not so much come into existence under these conditions as it manifests an existence that was always already there. This was one of the hypotheses generated by Walter Benjamin as a result of his hashish experiments:

> When we are conversing with someone and at the same time can see the person we are talking to smoking his cigar or walking around the room and so on, we feel no surprise that despite the effort we are making to speak to him, we are still able to follow his movements. The situation is quite different when the images we have before

us while speaking to someone have their origin in ourselves. In a normal state of consciousness, this is of course quite impossible. Or rather, such images do arise—they may even arise constantly—but they remain unconscious. It is otherwise with hashish intoxication. As this very evening proved, there can be an absolutely blizzard-like production of images, independently of whether our attention is directed toward anyone or anything else. Whereas in our normal state free-floating images to which we pay no heed simply remain in the unconscious, under the influence of hashish images present themselves to us seemingly without requiring our attention. Of course, this process may result in the production of images that are so extraordinary, so fleeting, and so rapidly generated that we can do nothing but gaze at them simply because of their beauty and singularity. (*On Hashish* 59–60)[9]

Hashish, that is, makes one aware of images that are clearly allied to those of hypnagogia—images that Benjamin suggests have always been playing just below the surface of consciousness, though overlaid and obscured by perceptions from without.

A similar hypothesis is generated by a very different experience in Alex Garland's 2004 novel *The Coma*. Its protagonist, Carl, is thrown into a coma after a vicious beating. He awakens in the hospital, but only after he returns home does he realize that he has lost various aspects of his memory, including any notion of *how* he got home. Eventually he realizes that the reality he is inhabiting, for all its intense detail, is a hallucinatory one. After another awakening into another reality, he realizes that he has never awakened at all, and is still in the coma. He now embarks on a search for the missing pieces of his memory, which he hopes will trigger a genuine awakening. At one point he feels himself beginning to rise toward the surface, only to sink back again to the deepest level yet: a place of complete darkness where he is disembodied, merely "consciousness, suspended in a void" (151). Moreover, he realizes that this is what he is at the core, whether waking or dreaming: "Strip down my waking life, and I'm a consciousness in a void. Strip down my dream life, and I'm a consciousness in a void" (159). The breakdown of the distinctions between waking and dreaming leads to another kind of breakdown, which Carl describes as "losing your mind" (152). This breakdown is characterized by certain understandable feelings of despair and fear—but also, peculiarly, by a flood of loud (and thus capitalized) words, terrifying in their incoherence:

> BENT UNION TRACK OVER FINE CUBA ORE UNDER RED SORT
> ETHER INK TOKE INTRO SATURN NILE OR TRAP AMPS SECT
> REVS AVE. . . . (153)

This is in fact a kind of verbal hypnagogia, a discharge flickering madly among its various nodal words. After Carl wakes from this, though only into what he knows is still a hallucinatory reality, he hears these strings of words again, with a difference: "Oddly, though the words seemed less random than before, I think they had less meaning" (175). The third time he hears the words is at the very moment when he truly awakes from his coma. As Carl rises toward the surface, this flood of flickering words is not left behind but accompanies him even as he opens his eyes. By implication it has always accompanied him, an ongoing obbligato to his consciousness. Significantly, as they move toward the surface the words have become more grammatical, so that at this threshold moment they *almost* make sense. They are the last words of the book, and they partake of both realms, the dream world and the waking one:

> INSIDE WHAT ORDER KEPT EVENING UNDER PROTECTION
> AGAINST NEW DUST IT TRIES WARNING ALL SEASONS AND
> LIGHTS LANTERNS AROUND DEVILS REACHES ECHOES ARE
> MADE. (200)

While this is not Joycean prose, it does suggest something about Joyce's language, or any language: that it has its origins in an unconscious that it both evokes and covers over. So something dies, according to Carl, at the moment of waking: "When you wake, you lose a narrative, and you never get it back" (200). This lost dream narrative exists in a mode that can only be crudely approximated by our morning-after recountings. On the other hand, every literary narrative flickers at its edges with unpredictable associations. Any page of a novel is a threshold zone, whose words simultaneously partake of the waking and the dreaming worlds. Alvarez's suggestion that hypnagogia poses a fundamental challenge to literature should itself be challenged: for some version of hypnagogic play is involved in any literary experience.

THE OBBLIGATO EFFECT

Sometimes the link to hypnagogia can become explicit. At the opening of Italo Svevo's *Confessions of Zeno,* for instance, Zeno describes himself writing the pages that will follow, and is pulled up short by an odd intrusion: while writing,

> I dimly see certain strange images that have no connection with my past; an engine puffing up a steep incline dragging endless coaches. Where can it all come from? Where is it going? How did it get there in the first place? (29–30)

How, indeed? While this is a question beyond the scope of this study, it is at least clear that Zeno's images are hypnagogic. The hypnagogic connection is strengthened by Zeno's comment, just before this passage, that on the previous night he had tried to let himself go completely—that is, yield to the hypnagogic images—and rather typically had succeeded only in falling asleep. "But today," he says, "this pencil will prevent my going to sleep" (29). The act of writing, then, holds Zeno on a borderline similar to that between waking and dreaming, the very locus in which hypnagogia manifests itself.

We can find a similar example of a writer being surprised by an image if we return to *The Gray Book.* Fioretos at one point is seeking the most suitable Latin word for weeping and comes down strongly for *ululare:*

> To taste the word is to experience how it sticks in a throat thick with hesitation, *huh,* before it begins to disentangle itself, *uh huh,* from its shelter of shyness, eking out of its reserve, and then begins to roll on, *uh huh huh,* without rein or restraint . . . *uh huh huhlare . . . uh huh hulare . . .* (Quick image of scrawny cogwheels on which, one by one, the eye's warm drops of amber oil are falling.) (45)

Neither weeping nor Latin interests me in this curious passage, except as it leads up to that "quick image." Actually it is no quicker than many of the other images with which Fioretos lards his eccentric treatise; it is less quick, for instance, than the "shelter of shyness" preceding the more lengthily described parenthetical image. If the description is lengthy, however, the image is not: it is a mere visual flicker that accompanies and emerges from the words attempting to give the "taste" of this one word *ululare*. Fioretos puts it in parentheses because it emerged not in the text but in his mind's eye while he was writing.

Perhaps this image is not so clearly hypnagogic as the one in Svevo, but neither can it be definitively separated from the hypnagogic realm. Both images remind us of the degree to which writing always takes place in a liminal zone, neither wholly on the page nor wholly in the mind. The mind, moreover, draws words out of another kind of liminal zone, one that Maurice Blanchot has repeatedly attempted to do justice to, and often in terms of image. For instance:

> Writing begins only when it is the approach to that point where nothing reveals itself, where, at the heart of dissimulation, speaking is still but the shadow of speech, a language which is still only its image, an imaginary language and a language of the imaginary, the one nobody speaks, the murmur of the incessant and interminable which one has to *silence* if one wants, at last, to be heard. (*Space* 48)

One silences this murmur, paradoxically, with words, which are set in place over what is incessant and interminable rather as a rock is placed over the entrance to a tomb. But never with complete success. The shadowy realm behind words, out of which words emerged, itself emerges around the edges of our conscious attention. So if, while writing, one fleetingly sees overburdened engines or cogwheels propelled by oily tears, it becomes evident that something is present in writing besides an author's own desired communication. Although such images cannot wholly usurp an author's claim to mastery, to being the source of what gets written, they are without a doubt involved with the elusive process that generates words on a page.

Genetic critics try to retrieve something of this process through examining the drafts, notes, and even doodles that came before the received text. Of course, as Jean Bellemin-Noël has admitted, "this ensemble is not always all there is (whatever could be formulated in thought without being written on paper is missing, at any rate)" (31).

And we might go even further to wonder whether "thought" is always that which can be formulated. So genetic critics themselves admit that they can go only so far in capturing the fleeting associations that precede any text, while never making it to its surface, or even that of its earliest drafts. Still less can we detect such associations through the examination of a text's "imagery." This venerable method employs, all too often, a kind of connect-the-dots approach: individual instances found in the text are joined with others until, if you are lucky, they emerge as a symbol, conscious and intended by the author. What is not fully conscious and textually realized—the true *avant-texte,* as genetic critics refer to it—is lost. Yet this matter is not mere waste, the *disjecta membra* of a certain body of work. In writing, sentences generate sentences. They do this through an associative process in which each sentence offers a field of possibilities, only a few of which are realized in the sentence that follows. That is to say, anyone who is writing is at the same time reading; and authors reading their own words may experience unexpected associations, as demonstrated in Fioretos's case. Fioretos, however, is quite exceptional in the attention he pays to the mental reactions that accompany the reading of his own writing, and in his willingness to record those in words. Most authors are well beyond any possibility of retrieving this nebulous process, even for themselves, and certainly for anyone else. If, then, we want to find out something about the associations that flicker behind a text, it is not to authors we should turn but to ourselves. We must reexamine our own experiences of reading.

Blanchot, who has written extensively and rigorously on writing, has much less to say about reading. In contrast to the agonies of writing, he says, reading is "a light, innocent Yes" (*Space* 196). And this is so even though reading enacts a passage "from the world where everything has more or less meaning, where there is obscurity and clarity, into a space where, properly speaking, nothing has meaning yet, toward which nevertheless everything which does have meaning returns as toward its origin" (196). He does not link this ambiguous space of literature with the ambiguities of image, which he extensively analyzes elsewhere ("Two Versions of the Imaginary" in *Space,* esp. 263). Yet the aim of authors is often—as Joseph Conrad famously puts it in the preface to *The Nigger of the Narcissus*—"above all to make you *see*" (14). This does not, of course, guarantee that readers will see the same things that the author saw while imagining the fictional scene, nor even that they will be exclusively focused on doing so. Even as the author is telling us what to see, and so encouraging us to look *through* the signifier at a specified image, that very signifier has a material component that encourages modes of seeing quite different from the one Conrad is referring to: homographs, anagrams, words closely but differently spelled, puns that are heard more than seen—the associations that accompany reading may be extremely varied. Here I will be dealing neither with the ways we see the printed page nor with the ways we see past the page to construct sustained imaginative visions in Conrad's sense.[10] Rather, I want to pay attention to images that flicker so briefly at the borders of reading that we are scarcely aware of them. To some degree they are repressed during the process of constructing meaning while reading, because they are judged to be irrelevant to that process. They are nevertheless part of the *experience* of reading, which comprehends more than textual comprehension. If reading performs certain meaning-making functions, it also has aspects that do not directly contribute to those functions and might for that reason be considered dysfunctional. Let's take a look at representative examples of both functional and dysfunctional aspects. I will begin with mental images presented as functional.

In *Dreaming by the Book*, Elaine Scarry has explained that what authors do is to guide the reader's image making in such a way as to mimic the processes by which perceptions combine to make up a world; authors *instruct* their readers on what they should pay attention to, even if the specifics of that attention remain to be filled in. Scarry offers as an example of this practice the opening paragraph of *Tess of the d'Urbervilles*,[11] restoring and making explicit the implicit imperatives:

> On an evening in the latter part of May *[picture this]* a middle-aged man was walking homeward from Shaston to the village of Marlott, in the adjoining Vale of *[hear the names]* Blackmore or Blackmoor. *[Look closely at the walker's legs.]* The pair of legs that carried him

were rickety, and there was a bias in his gait which inclined him somewhat to the left of a straight line. *[Let your eyes drift up to his face now.]* He occasionally gave a smart nod, as if in confirmation of some opinion, *[drift now to the region of his skull]* though he was not thinking of anything in particular. *[Look, now, at his arm: tell us what you see so we know you are actually looking at his arm.]* An empty egg-basket was slung upon his arm. *[Picture a second person.]* Presently he was met by an elderly parson *[look closely at his legs]* astride on a *[look closely at the color]* gray mare, who, as he rode, *[hear the sounds coming now]* hummed a wandering tune. *[Hear a voice saying]* 'Good night t'ee,' *[and look to see who it comes from]* said the man with the basket. (36–37)

Here is another reader reading the same passage and blithely disregarding these directions:

On an evening in the latter part of May *[Keats in the dark]* a middle-aged man was walking homeward from Shaston *[a bright spike]* to the village of Marlott *[ominous purple]*, in the adjoining Vale *[like Windermere]* of Blackmore or Blackmoor *[Blackamoor? No, Blackmore. Why two names?]*/*[valley of the shadow]*. The pair of legs that carried him *[quick image of self-propelling legs shading into a shapeless bundle on top, probably derived from* Codex Seraphinianus *image]* were rickety *[rickets?/open slats of a leaning shed]*, and there was a bias in his gait *[gaiters on the legs]* which inclined him somewhat to the left of a straight line *[mathematical diagram]*/*[There was a crooked man]*. He occasionally gave a smart nod, as if in confirmation of some opinion, though he was not thinking of anything in particular *[tic? Senile jerks?]*. An empty egg-basket *[sense of an airy hemisphere surrounded by wicker]* was slung *[it becomes a bit heavier]* upon his arm. *[To market, to market]* Presently he was met by an elderly parson astride *[riding to Canterbury]* on a gray mare *[the old g.m., she ain't what she used to be]*, who, as he rode, hummed a wandering *[wandering willy]* tune *[faint trace of an aimless line]*. 'Good night t'ee,' *[?? =To yee. Yee?]* said the man with the basket.

This other reader is, of course, me; and this experiment in self-reflection (and self-exposure) attempts to record as accurately and honestly as possible associations that do *not* follow the straight line but incline toward wandering. The italicized associations are not likely to be anything you would "agree" with or declare to be "right." To be sure, there may be some associations that other readers might share—I do not claim to be extraordinary—but other associations are peculiar to me, or just plain peculiar. Many of them reflect my previous experiences in reading; they are a subtle version of inter-textuality. Some might be categorized as phenomenological and go beyond what is licensed by the language; others are focused on the materiality of the print. Sometimes two very different associations can unfold at the same time, or nearly the same time; I have tried to signal this simultaneity with slash marks.

While we now have two very different versions of what goes on when we read, they are not incompatible with each other; they are perfectly capable of going on at the same time. Scarry's version suffers, perhaps, from its painstaking itemization of the obvious—though I concede that "the obvious" is often just a name for what is most commonly overlooked. My version suffers from the opposite fault, of being irresponsible, quirky, and at times downright silly. I take heart, however, from Wittgenstein's observation that "if people did not sometimes do silly things, nothing intelligent would ever get done."[12] What I am trying to get done here is to gain some new insight into how readers interact with a text, how they bring associations with them that are quickened by the words of the text in an embarrassment of riches. It is . . . well, obvious that people's associations are not always profound or, *pace* Freud, meaningful. And this is as true in reading as elsewhere. Yet, as I hope to show, these superfluous associations have their uses, and their pleasures.

In Scarry's model, the text is pedagogical; it instructs us in what to do at any moment. A "good" reader will dutifully follow directions; another kind of reader—shall we call this a "bad" reader?—will follow indirections to find directions out. For instance, take my own set of indirections, given above: if we ignore some of the more aberrant swings there is a certain consistency in the texture of associations. And is it absolutely beyond the pale to detect in Hardy's quaint country world reminiscences of nursery-rhyme figures, the Wordsworthian common man, and even perhaps a Chaucerian pilgrim?

While such reminiscences cannot be described as allusions, and therefore be enlisted in a project of conscious control by the author and the "good reader," they may in fact add to the scene's *vivacity*. Here I am shamelessly stealing Scarry's term for the vivid mimesis of perception through following the author's instructions. I want to stretch *vivacity* to include not just what we see but how we feel about what we see, what we almost see behind what we do see, associations clinging to the images that present themselves to us. Indeed, this is always an important aspect of seeing, though it is usually occluded by the sheer material impress of perceptual stimuli. In *imaginative* seeing, this aspect moves into the foreground, whether it is rendered explicitly on the printed page or not. Even as a reader follows the implied directive to "see this" or "see that," the specifics of what is then seen will always be drawn from a memory bank of personal images. Such images, precisely because they are personal, will never be free of associations; and what is associated with them may well be other images. Some of these will be no more meaningful than static on the radio; others will contribute to an effect of intimacy that is no small part of the pleasure of reading; all are part of a process of meaning making that always comprehends more than any particular meaning made.

The nature of that "more" is the focus of Daniel Dennett's multiple-draft theory of consciousness. Consciousness, for Dennett, is never a fixed fact but always a process, a process of multiple drafts. And this must be true as well of any of its meaning-making activities, such as reading. The writing metaphor here—multiple drafts—should not lead us to assume that we have a chronological progression from the "rough draft" to the finished product, the definitive reading; as Dennett states, "There is no privileged finish line, so the temporal order of experience cannot be what fixes the subjective order in experience" (*Consciousness Explained* 119). There is a temporal order, of course—consciousness does not abolish time—but it is only "something like" sequence, for a complex simultaneity characterizes what Dennett describes as a "multitrack process":

> This multitrack process occurs over hundreds of milliseconds, during which time various additions, incorporations, emendations, and overwritings of content can occur, in various orders. These yield,

over the course of time, something rather like a narrative stream or
sequence, which can be thought of as subject to continual editing
by many processes distributed around in the brain, and continuing
indefinitely into the future. Contents arise, get revised, contribute to
the interpretation of other contents or to the modulation of behavior
(verbal and otherwise). . . . This skein of contents is only rather like
a narrative because of its multiplicity; at any point in time there are
multiple drafts of narrative fragments at various stages of editing in
various places in the brain. (135)

That is to say, as consciousness makes meaning—including the
meaning of a text—it casts an extraordinarily wide net. What wonder,
then, if it brings up not only the Meaning of the White Whale but also
an innumerable host of small fry, flickering and brightly colored? For
meaning to be made at all, consciousness must in the first instance
resort to the meaningless, enter a realm where, in Blanchot's phrase,
"nothing has meaning *yet*" (*Space* 196; emphasis mine). It must sift
through associations and connections that may be entirely random
before discarding some, retaining others. And again I must stress
that the process is not one of steady refinement, since drafts at an
advanced stage may be yet be discarded, and elements that have been
discarded may be retrieved and fitted into yet another draft.

Reading, then, is never wholly the "light, innocent Yes" that
Blanchot suggests it is, never an effortless acquiescence to the author's instructions. However blithely we are skimming over the surface, we are allowing that surface to stir up our depths (which is not
to say our profundities: as I have already observed, deeply buried associations may often be trivial or banal). Our absorption in the words
on the page is never, can never be, complete; our attention often
wanders, and does so arbitrarily, not just in order to gather material
that will contribute to an aesthetic meaning. This wandering differs,
then, from Wolfgang Iser's notion of the "wandering viewpoint," for
that is a "synthesizing process . . . which will lead to the formation of
the aesthetic object" (109–10). While the aesthetic object is no doubt
constructed by such a synthesizing process, there are other processes
that may be going on at the same time. These are not so task ori-
ented; they do not wander merely as a preliminary to settling down,

but create—to steal a phrase from Hardy's page—their own "wandering tune."[13]

Let me give that tune a name: *obbligato,* a term that I have already used in passing but that now deserves a more extended meditation. The Italian word originally referred to a musical line that the performer was "obliged" to play exactly as written. In a score, it signaled a departure from the common practice, in the baroque period, of notating the keyboard part as a figured bass to be filled out ad lib. As the written-out obbligato sections were often designed to provide a countermelody to the music's main line, the term gradually reversed itself and came to mean something very much like an ad-lib improvisation around the main theme. Of course, with the written score becoming increasingly paramount in the modern period, an obbligato part is no longer ad lib but a part of the score as given: the most familiar example is probably the piccolo obbligato in Sousa's march *The Stars and Stripes Forever.* Only in jazz can we find something like a truly improvised obbligato, often around a previously stated but currently absent melody. The term *obbligato,* then, has antithetical meanings, like the ones that Freud found in primal words.

This antithesis carries over into the "wandering tune" that forms an obbligato around the words of a literary text. On one hand, a reader, while following the story line as (tacitly) instructed, will freely embroider that line with associations that are nothing if not ad lib. On the other hand, this is something that a reader is always "obliged" to do; the associations arise in the mind unbidden, so that it is almost never possible to read at the denotative level alone, even assuming that that was what the author intended us to do in the first place. If at times we do seem to be reading at that level, it is because the associative obbligato is always a provisional one, part of a series of rapid-fire draftings most of which will be discarded. Not until the reader's consciousness has settled on a draft that has an acceptable affinity with the text is the association admitted into full consciousness, if only provisionally. This implies, of course, that most of our associations with a literary text are errors. Certainly they are so etymologically, since *error* derives from the Latin *errare,* to wander; the word is often used in this sense in early modern poetry. And an ad-lib or arbitrary association may solidify into an unequivocal error of judgment if it can be demonstrated to be at odds with what is stated on the page. But most such associations will remain within a flickering liminal zone, where they are part of the trial-and-error process that is involved in any meaning making.

They are also, I would argue, part of the pleasure of the text. Roland Barthes at one point makes a move in this direction:

> My pleasure can very well take the form of a drift. *Drifting* occurs whenever *I do not respect the whole,* and whenever, by dint of seeming driven about by language's illusions, seductions, and intimidations, like a cork on the waves, I remain motionless, pivoting on the *intractable* bliss that binds me to the text. (*Pleasure of the Text* 18)

The "intractable" here *(intraitable),* we may hazard, is that which does not follow the line of the text, does not obey its instructions. Rather, while remaining motionless as far as furthering the text's motion is concerned, it pivots (pivoting is also a motion) within the reader's own stimulated associations. The result is a bliss, however subliminal, like that of the "writerly" text, as the mind takes off in its own indirections, writing a countermelody to the text's overt themes. Such are the pleasures of merely circulating, to borrow the title of Wallace Stevens's poem.

Nor does it matter all that much that these motions of the mind are barely admitted to consciousness. For when we read, we are aware not only of the shapes of phrases and sentences, not only of the particular "meaning" that words like nets enmesh, but also of the associative reticulations of our own minds. As words are registered in certain areas of the brain, metabolism in those areas increases: they will "light up" on a scan produced by neuroimaging techniques. This is not to say that everything is brought into the light. Researchers carrying out early neuroimaging studies reported "some degree of surprise at finding activation in brain regions not traditionally believed to be implicated in language processing. . . . Since then, these findings have been replicated and extended in a number of studies, identifying a wide range of regions of activation during word processing" (Gernsbacher and Kaschak 96). What happens during reading, then, may well go beyond what happens when a specific task is focused on by both the subjects and the researchers. If "increasing task difficulty can lead to the activation of more diffuse brain regions" (Gernsbacher and Kaschak 104), an evocative and complex work of literature is likely to involve the brain in ways that are both more microscopic and more widely interwoven than a brain scan can at present capture. Brain imaging cannot account for everything that is activated. As words pass over them, certain areas of the brain light up, to be sure too quickly in most cases for us to see clearly what is being illuminated. But the nerve endings have been brushed during consciousness's continual work of selection and rejection. And even what is rejected—which is most of it—is a part of us, a part that has briefly been called out of oblivion and into . . . obscurity. Obscurely we sense our own riches, moving beneath the surface of words, of recognized meanings. There is a pleasure in this that is not, strictly speaking, the pleasure of the text but something that has been evoked in us *by* the text and exists, as it were, to the side of it.

In his essay "Pleasure and Self-Loss in Reading," Barry Weller speaks on behalf of "those less than articulate, almost preconscious, sources of pleasure of which most theoretical models of reading give small account" (10). I am trying to remedy this shortcoming, adding one more theoretical model of reading to those we already have. But that model may also illuminate what is going on in certain kinds of *writing*, modes that draw their pleasure, and their power, from this liminal zone of rapid-fire association. It is not news that writing of this kind predominates in poetry. However, it is not generally recognized that novels may also be designed to evoke this zone, at least at intervals. In certain passages, metaphors seem to break free of their assigned duty of focusing and vivifying the meaning being communicated. Instead they stray, loosen, and unfurl with a life of their own. This does not mean that such a passage is a flaw or interruption in the text, even though it may interrupt the story line. That "life of their own," that obbligato that accompanies not only a text but our own quotidian existence, may be the real subject of the text, beyond anything that can be conveyed by the sequence of events. Near the beginning of *Nightwood*, for instance, Djuna Barnes describes Robin

Vote, within four pages, in the following ways (I have truncated the descriptions where possible, and where this was not possible have quoted directly):

1. fungi
2. sea amber
3. plant life
4. "as if sleep were a decay fishing her beneath the visible surface"
5. phosphorus
6. a painting by Rousseau *(The Dream)*
7. "an eland coming down an aisle of trees, chapleted with orange blossoms and bridal veil"
8. the unicorn
9. "the converging halves of a broken fate, setting face, in sleep, toward itself in time, as an image and its reflection in a lake seem parted only by the hesitation in the hour"
10. the "aside" of an actor (34–37)

While these associations circle around Robin Vote, their sheer range provides a pleasure that takes off tangentially and goes well beyond the pleasure of an introduction, or even of an obsession. Admittedly *Nightwood* is an extreme example, though not the unique aberration it is sometimes claimed to be. Barnes is representative of a certain school of writing that is deliberately overwrought, that plays dangerously with dandification and excess, that hovers at the edges of language. Its authors may be as various as Thomas De Quincey and Norman Mailer, Thomas Carlyle and Severo Sarduy. But even in novels less extreme than *Nightwood* such obbligato passages may be found, to various degrees, and they have similar effects.

A novel that is particularly concerned with the obbligatos that accompany our consciousness is Virginia Woolf's *The Waves*, from which the following passage is taken:

> But it is a mistake, this extreme precision, this orderly and military progress; a convenience, a lie. There is always deep below it, even when we arrive punctually at the appointed time with our white waistcoats and polite formalities, a rushing stream of broken dreams, nursery rhymes, street cries, half-finished sentences and

sights—elm trees, willow trees, gardeners sweeping, women writing—that rise and sink even as we hand a lady down to dinner. While one straightens the fork so precisely on the table-cloth, a thousand faces mop and mow. There is nothing one can fish up in a spoon; nothing one can call an event. Yet it is alive too and deep, this stream. (255–56)

This is Bernard speaking, during the long last section in which he sums up his life, and the novel. Bernard is a failed writer because he is so immersed in this stream, so aware of it, that he cannot really believe in stories, with their claims to "event" and meaningful structure. If he begins a story it fizzles out at the end; all he can bring up is phrases, however brilliant these might be. It is the way he is made, and he has known this almost from the beginning. An earlier passage:

The bubbles are rising like the silver bubbles from the floor of a saucepan; image on top of image. I cannot sit down to my book, like Louis, with ferocious tenacity. I must open the little trap-door and let out these linked phrases in which I run together whatever happens so that instead of incoherence there is perceived a wandering thread, lightly joining one thing to another. (49)

What has begun as a recital of his shortcomings has ended in a cautious affirmation. While Bernard cannot believe in stories with their neat sequences, he senses that there are other ways of "joining one thing to another," of making connections. Indeed, it is only by virtue of wandering that a thread of coherence can emerge at all. Bernard is of course an aspect of Virginia Woolf herself, who was constantly haunted by the possibility of failure and famously opposed the idea of life as a "series of gig-lamps, symmetrically arranged" by authors ("Modern Fiction" 106). Bernard's last sentence indeed describes the method of *The Waves*, where "event" is relegated to the sidelines and the novel's protagonists deliver themselves of monologues that they would never in fact have spoken in this way, perhaps not even to themselves. Yet through these monologues—their richly interwoven perceptions, perceptions that become metaphors, metaphors that rhythmically recur—we sense in each case not a life's events but its distinctive *texture.*

In this, Woolf anticipates Nathalie Sarraute's later pursuit of those subtle inner movements that she calls *tropisms,* her lifelong preoccupation and subject matter. Sarraute acknowledges her debt to Woolf in the opening sentence of the essay "Conversation and Sub-conversation," though in a rather backhanded way: "Who today would dream of taking seriously, or even reading, the articles that Virginia Woolf wrote, shortly after the First World War, on the art of the novel?" (77). Only as the essay unfolds does it become apparent that the sentence is ironic, the ventriloquized voice of a contemporary prejudice against the moderns. Sarraute, while hardly arguing for a return to a modernist aesthetics, sees in work such as Woolf's the foundation of her own. For, she says, the reader of the modern novel

> was not long in perceiving what is hidden beneath the interior mono-
> logue: an immense profusion of sensations, images, sentiments,
> memories, impulses, little larval actions that no inner language can
> convey, that jostle one another on the threshold of consciousness. (91)[14]

While she then goes on to praise Proust for his attention to this realm, she also criticizes him for being overanalytical, for

> having incited the reader to use his own intelligence, instead of giv-
> ing him the sensation of reliving an experience, of accomplishing
> certain actions himself, without knowing too well what he is doing
> or where he is going—which always was and still is *in the very nature
> of any work of fiction.* (93; emphasis mine)

Shortly before this, she has described the traditional novel—*Tess of the d'Urbervilles* would fall into this category—as one in which read-ers "soon feel quite at home" (90). This would seem to contradict the uncertainty and errancy that Sarraute is now asserting to be part of any reader's experience of fiction. However, as shown by the ex-ercise I performed earlier on *Tess,* the "little larval actions . . . on the threshold of consciousness" exist here too, tropisms of the text. And theirs is hardly an analytical logic; rather, it is a trial-and-error associative process, most of which is discarded, never making its way to the surface of consciousness, where it can be amalgamated with the surface of the text. The distinctions that can be made between *Tess of the d'Urbervilles*, *Remembrance of Things Past*, *The Waves*, and Sarraute's own practice are then matters of degree, the degree to which the mind's obbligato may be foregrounded by the writer's technique. But in reading *any* fiction the mind must wander from the straight and narrow path of the printed line.

FALLING ASLEEP WHILE READING

Focused on our goals while reading—who dunnit, where is this going, what does it all mean—we tend to look past this wandering toward its ultimate product. And of course there is always the materiality of print on a page, with its implicit claim to deliver the information we need in order to carry on our project of making sense. There is little room for non-sense here, or at least little room to recognize the role that it always plays in reading. For the most part we recognize it only dimly, in passing. It can, however, emerge with a disconcerting power when our focused activity of hunting and gathering meaning slackens, entirely against our will, and we find that we are falling asleep over a book. As the liminal moment of hypnagogia suggests something about consciousness (which is not to be neatly separated from unconsciousness), so the moment when we fall asleep while reading suggests something about the way we always read, something overwritten, as it were, by the concerns of our waking mind. Yet little attention has been paid to what happens when our reading of a text slackens in this way—not by scientific researchers, and hardly at all by literary authors. From them, we have only a few near misses.

The narrator of Chaucer's "Book of the Duchess," troubled by insomnia, begins reading Ovid in bed. He chooses the tale of Seyes and Alcyone, which features a prayer for divine aid and an answer to that prayer granted in a dream. After finishing the tale, Chaucer's narrator imitates its actions, praying to a god (Morpheus, god of dreams, in this instance, rather than Hypnos, god of sleep) that he may finally overcome his long siege of wakefulness. The prayer is effective:

> ... sodeynly, I nyste how,
> Such a lust anoon me tooke
> To slepe that ryght upon my booke
> Y fil aslepe. (ll. 272–75)

What follows is a dream of waking, waking in a chamber that oddly contains the dreamer within textuality: "And alle the walles with colouris fyne / Were peynted, bothe text and glose / Of al the *Romaunce of the Rose*" (ll. 332–34). The colors indicate a pictorial rendition of the French work, not an uncommon medieval practice in aristocratic chambers; yet the addition of the "glose" or gloss moves us toward an implied material text, rather than its visualized subject matter. While there is within the dream, then, a certain persistence of the narrator's activity of reading, the actual moment of transition from reading to dream takes place too "sodeynly" for close observation.

The dream that is "Kubla Khan" has its genesis in a more precisely assigned moment of reading, as Coleridge explains in the prefatory note attached to the poem's first publication:

> [The author] fell asleep in his chair at the moment that he was reading the following sentence, or words of the same substance, in "Purchas's Pilgrimage": "Here the Khan Kubla commanded a palace to be built, and a stately garden thereunto. And thus ten miles of fertile ground were inclosed with a wall." (249)

With a poem so well known it is unnecessary to rehearse here the specific ways in which this sentence (or rather one like it in Purchas) impels the poem's composition, throwing up an ever-expanding series of images, images that are also things, things that are also words: "if that indeed can be called composition in which all the images rose up before him as *things*, with a parallel production of the correspondent expressions, without any sensation or consciousness of effort" (249–50). What is most important is to consider the source of this effect. It cannot be assigned wholly to the altered perceptions of the reading process produced by the onset of sleep, since the "two grains of opium taken to check a dysentery" (525) must also be taken into account. As Benjamin concludes in regard to his hashish experiments, a consciousness altered by drugs is not necessarily an unreliable informant about its own elusive processes. But it does mean that when Coleridge falls asleep there are forces other than those of sleep acting upon him, and the poem cannot then be taken as an unalloyed specimen of what goes on when one falls asleep while reading.

Marcel Proust comes close to giving us such a specimen as he begins *Remembrance of Things Past*. Here are its opening sentences:

> For a long time I went to bed early. Sometimes, my candle scarcely out, my eyes would close so quickly that I did not have time to say to myself: "I'm falling asleep." And, half an hour later, the thought that it was time to try to sleep would wake me; I wanted to put down the book I thought I still had in my hands, and blow out my light; I had not ceased while sleeping to form reflections on what I had just read, but these reflections had taken a rather peculiar turn; it seemed to me that I myself was what the book was talking about: a church, a quartet, the rivalry between François I and Charles V. This belief lived on for a few seconds after my waking; it did not shock my reason, but it lay heavy like scales on my eyes and kept them from realizing that the candlestick was no longer lit. Then it began to grow intelligible to me, as after metempsychosis do the thoughts of an earlier existence; the subject of my book detached itself from me, I was free to apply myself to it or not. (7)

We will be returning to this rich episode later, when considering the peculiarities of waking; but certainly its most peculiar part, in the narrator's own opinion, is his momentary feeling that he has become what he was reading about. There is some kinship here, perhaps, with Georges Poulet's observations:

> I am someone who happens to have as objects of his own thought, thoughts which are part of a book I am reading, and which are therefore the cogitations of another. They are the thoughts of another, and yet it is I who am their subject. The situation is even more astonishing than the one noted above. I am thinking the thoughts of another. Of course, there would be no cause for astonishment if I were thinking it as the thought of another. But I think it as my very own. . . . My consciousness behaves as though it were the consciousness of another. (44)

Leaving aside the obbligato with which our own thoughts, or rather associations, accompany the thoughts of another (temporarily our own), something "even more astonishing" than Poulet's phenomenon is being described by Proust. For he does not say that in his sleep he continued to think about the rivalry between François I and Charles V, but rather that "I myself *was*" that rivalry, which is quite a different thing. It is indeed hard to imagine what it would be like to be neither François I nor Charles V but the rivalry between them, and perhaps such a thing is possible only within the peculiar logic of dream. So we have here not a continuation of Marcel's reading process in sleep but a morphing of it. Reading is reshaped to become simultaneously the matter being treated by the book before it was interrupted by the swift onset of sleep and something else, the nature of which we must now try to determine.

Let's begin again with almost the same sentence, which then goes in a rather different direction:

> For a long time I used to go to bed early. Though the art of reading is not widespread in these parts, I confess myself to be a devotee of the practice and, in particular, of reading in bed. It is peculiarly pleasant, I have found, to lie with the book propped up against the knees and, feeling the lids grow heavy, to drift off to sleep, to drift off in such a way that in the morning it seems unclear where the burden of the book ended and my own dreams began. (11)

This is the opening of *The Arabian Nightmare,* by Robert Irwin, which I will be taking up at greater length later on. At this point Irwin's rewriting of Proust serves to emphasize the liminal state toward which the preceding examples have been gradually moving. It provides our most explicit example of the fusion of the dreaming and waking states at the page's surface, where it is "unclear where the burden of the book ended and my own dreams began." Perhaps it must always be, has always been, unclear. But we become aware of this only at liminal moments like those that Proust and Irwin describe, and that we may sometimes experience. What is that experience like?

I am in bed, with my book propped up before me, and I am falling asleep while reading. A dim sense of drowsiness has started to envelop me like a soft down, and so I promise myself to put the book away after I finish this chapter. Only a few paragraphs to go. But the sentences seem to slow and open, their neat dovetailing giving way to rich implications. I sense all kinds of connections to what I am already familiar with from earlier in the book. Oddly enough, these connections continue to connect, only now with each other. They are making an intense kind of sense, familiar now not from the book but from somewhere else, perhaps my own life, or perhaps this is only something I dreamed. I'm losing track. My eyes focus and I realize that the narrative I am following is not the one on the page. I force myself to stare at the actual words. I see them as material shapes that I know, with meanings that go with those shapes, but they seem oddly disconnected, like exercises in a foreign language. I push myself to read them as coherent sentences. After a torpid start, the sentences recover their ability to flow together, and to carry me along in a swirl of eloquence—to the very moment when my book lands heavily on my stomach, waking me at the very threshold of sleep.

Such moments bring to the foreground a background that has always been necessary for our reading. Intellectually, no doubt, we have always known that reading takes place as much in the spaces between words as it does by means of the words themselves. In the experience described above, the words actually appear, if only momentarily, as the mechanical constructions they always were, each with its own assigned meanings. And the spaces between reveal themselves as not really "spaces" at all, but areas teeming with movement: images, incipient relationships, narrative fragments, drafts of meaning that can, if highly charged enough, become drifts, seducing the reader away from a "responsible" reading of the text. "In reading," Philippe Sollers has said, "we must become aware of what we write unconsciously by our reading" (*Logiques* 220). Only through such a writing is reading possible at all. Yet it is the most elusive of realms, for it takes place at the very borders of consciousness, the place where consciousness is taken over by something else that thinks otherwise than do our daylight minds. We catch a glimpse of it, sometimes, just as we edge over into sleep—though, as Danilo Kiš's narrator finds, it is the most difficult thing in the world to grasp that liminal space. Yet we must learn to inhabit this realm, one akin to the gray vagueness that is Fioretos's subject matter: "So this will be our realm. Between sign and significance. Or gesture and gist. Made of a vagueness lazily lasting like mist" (19).[15] And it is no doubt significant that the locus in which he finds this realm most often is "in bed" (19).

AGATHA: OR, SLEEP

On January 15, 1898, Paul Valéry wrote to André Gide, describing the inception of a story that was fated never to get much past its inception. Valéry even knew this at the time, describing the story as something that "I shall never finish because it's too difficult" (*Poems in the Rough* 316). It was to deal with a woman in a sort of cataleptic sleep lasting for years. Assuming that our dreams feed off of the memories of our waking lives, Valéry's original project was to study "the impoverishment or dwindling (or whatever) of the datum on which she fell asleep" (316). This seems to have changed, as time went on, into a simpler project: to render the stages of a normal night's sleep, though viewed through the consciousness of an unusually aware woman. That project proved to be not at all simple, and it never progressed beyond the description of sleep's initial onset; even this was beset with problems. Valéry returned intermittently to this work, which he usually referred to as *Agatha*. Other titles he considered were *Agatha: Or, Sleep* and, in homage to Edgar Allan Poe, *Manuscript Found in a Brain*. He finally abandoned the project definitively around 1903.

Agatha has a place in Valéry's ongoing attempt to establish a physics of the mind. Introduced to the principles of thermodynamics when he attended a series of lectures given at the Sorbonne in 1900 (Miura 84), Valéry found in the notion of the *phase* an illuminating way to approach his own concerns about the nature of consciousness. Just as the material world can move through phases of solid, liquid, and gas, so consciousness can enact different phases of itself, and indeed can do so at concurrent times; consciousness is a continuum that comprises a variety of states. So sleep is a phase of consciousness worth investigating, and comprises within itself a number of phases. The transitions between such phases were always of interest to Valéry: one of his notebooks was titled *Somnia*, and he repeatedly wrote about the nature of sleep, dream, waking, and insomnia. *Agatha* was a sustained attempt—even if Valéry could not sustain it—to trace the phases of sleep.

"The more I think, the more I think"—the opening sentence of *Agatha*—might well describe the restless proliferation of thoughts in insomnia, but here there is no anxiety over wakefulness, for the speaker is poised on the edge of sleep: "I am changing in shadow, in a bed" (*Poems in the Rough* 205).[16] So the multiplication of thoughts is witnessed with an odd detachment: "Yes, ever newer I see all known things within me become astonishing, and afterward still more known. Suddenly I have slowly conceived them: when they vanish, they do it easily" (205). There is paradox and contradiction here, but Agatha's state of mind accepts all that as natural enough. Her eyes, still open, see in the darkness otherwise than in the light. All unfolds with a minimal effort, transforming the remains of the day: "No more than adequate, it maintains amid the busy shade an exiguous remnant of the glittering day—day thought of, and thinking almost. This paltry glimmer resolves into a dull and fleeting cheek, a pointless face soon smiling against me, responsive, itself consumed by luster-swallowing dusk." This face, so fleeting, is a hypnagogic image; and others accompany Agatha as she sinks further into sleep: "The darkness fathers forth a few scraps still, of a flimsy seascape, ruffles them, and the icy crupper of a horse" (206).

But these images against the darkness are also described as words. At first this is done somewhat ambiguously:

> Upon this sophistical shadow I scrawl, as if with phosphorus, the fading formulas I need; and when I reach the end, near the point of their resumption, I must always trace them out again, for the more I nourish them the deeper they sleep, before I come to change them. (207)

A bit later, as Agatha engages with the question of who this "I" is and whether she is truly the agent of these fading formulas, she is led to ask, "WHO is asking?" And answers: "The same who replies. The same who writes, effacing a same line. They are but writings on water." These are metaphors, but they are hardly innocent ones, for they remind us that it is writing that we are reading now. And since metaphors are always departures from literal truth, they throw into doubt whether words on a page can really convey the experience that Agatha is having—a doubt that, as he confided to Gide, plagued Valéry from the start.

If these are "but writings on water," that water, as it is described between the two quotations, becomes the medium of the self's dissolution, the drowning in doubt that impels Agatha to ask, "WHO is asking?" Within her, the solid world has entered a liquid phase; and she compares her state to

> swimming with wet eyes, abundance of flexible indolence with feet floating in the fullness of high water. . . . Human, almost upright in the coiled spring of the sea, swathed in enormous cold, upon whom the whole hugeness weighs, even to his shoulders, even to his ears despoiled of variable noise, I still touch the strange absence of soil. (206)

This description evokes the sensation of indolence that accompanies the approach of sleep, a sensation that is not without its elements of terror. Sleep has not yet claimed Agatha, as indicated by her paradoxical awareness of the absence of soil as something that can be touched. And she knows that "yet icier deeps, concealed below, forgo me but will mount again to drink me in some dream" (207). The image of a swimmer recurs in Valéry's notebooks: "I wake up like a swimmer resurfacing," he says at one point (*Cahiers* 3:428). Yet perhaps one never resurfaces entirely, for there are disconcerting similarities between Agatha's liminal state and the waking state as Valéry describes it: "We *are*, as though by constantly maintained action, like the movement of a swimmer having to tread water to stay afloat" (*Cahiers* 3:439). The liquid phase of one's psychology is always present beneath the apparent solidity of the present moment—which moreover is never wholly present. Repeatedly Valéry describes the waking state as one that is always partially elsewhere, one that occludes certain elements of the perceptual world in order to better make its choices, choices made in accordance with certain frameworks of thought that are not themselves present. "Mental life in waking is," he says, "a continual suppression or repression of the attempt to go beyond" (*Cahiers* 3:427). In dreams we have a "combination by EVERY POSSIBLE MEANS of diverse impressions. The waking state combines only what is compatible with the prevailing system" (*Cahiers* 3:421). This is an act of will and attention by the waking self; will, certainly, is just what one must surrender in order to enter into sleep. Attention is more problematic: Valéry assigns the term *attention* at one moment to the waking world and at another moment to dream. Ultimately perhaps it is a matter of what one pays attention *to*. If the waking state consciously weighs factors that are found elsewhere than the present moment, that indicates a kind of inattention; yet those factors are being consciously weighed in their relation to "the prevailing system," which is the primary object of attention. In dreams things are quite different: "You no longer have the constant *choice* which characterizes waking" (*Cahiers* 3:418), and as a consequence your attention is exclusively paid to what is before you at the moment—which, to be sure, is in a continual state of flux. This state, this liquidity, "lives and flourishes in interludes that in the waking state do exist, but are extremely brief and rapidly corrected" (*Cahiers* 3:440). This observation has a certain affinity with Dennett's multiple-draft theory of consciousness, especially in the notion of correction according to a system of priorities that is consciously admitted to the attention.

Not yet wholly assimilated into dream, Agatha relinquishes that system of priorities:

> Gone is the unbroken watchfulness of the thread of awareness; no longer do I hear the endless murmur of the profound inexhaustible sibyl who calculates each particle of approaching futurity . . . , casting over the ensemble of unforced days a semblance of lucidity by her imperceptible preparation for their alterations. Now I experience no more cruxes of the within. All proceeds unamazedly, the springs of surprise run down. . . . Comprehension has no prey and no peculiar solidity distinguishes particular notions. (207–8)

If Agatha has moved closer to the world of dream in this way, she is not there yet: "This drift," she says, is "different from dream" (208), for she is held on the threshold of sleep by the street sounds that obtrude upon her:

> The tail-end of the town-noises penetrates my private sphere. It is the moment when all grows still and echoes thin away. The last changes are reckoned. An inordinate exterior region divests itself of existence. (208)

This dwindling of the external world makes itself known now through a distortion of the very noises that have bound her to it:

> Hearing expands to the very horizon, and it overhangs a gulf that grows immense. A continually more subtle creature leans over the void to catch the slightest sound; through her I plumb a space where the possible breathes and I fly! (208)

Not yet a flying dream, this is an impetus toward the certainty and fulfillment that dream holds out as its promise:

> I feel uncertainty speed from the forehead of time, the event arrive, its vigor, its languor, the dissolution of experience, and the rebirth of the voyage, as pure and hard as itself, adorned in unending mind. The new sheds itself in advance, by way of a shift more impercep-tible than the angle of the sky. (208–9)

It is here, at the critical moment of shifting into the world of sleep and dream, that Valéry begins to run into his real problems. At the edges of sleep, there has been enough left of Agatha's daylight consciousness to note what is happening to her, to describe the hyp-nagogic images, changes in her bodily sensations, and the balance between internal and external stimuli. Now that balance is begin-ning to tip over into modes that are so alien from daylight conscious-ness that they necessarily require explanation; yet to explain, rather than merely to accept, is to pull consciousness back into the world of waking reason. So Agatha illuminates the way that in dream "the new sheds itself in advance" by contrasting it with a self-knowledge that works in a very different way:

You can only know yourself in reverse. You carry *backward* a power,
a kind of discernment; and, being able to see only the opposite way
to the one you travel, you analyze what is finished, you act out only
what is done already. (209)

This is immediately followed by yet another contrast, carried out
through a backward look:

Once, I would reflect upon a magnificent number of subjects; but
now I am so peaceful that I seem to myself as if set apart, and suspended between this finite number and another whole mass, imminent but probably not in any connection with it. (209)

The once/but now distinction breaks down as soon as one realizes
that the preceding sentences are a consciously articulated reflection.
If the speaker is "set apart" it is not because Agatha is separated from
her habitual philosophizing. Rather, she is set apart from the very
state she is describing, by virtue of the difference between having
an experience and thinking what it might mean. It is a difference
that Valéry is entirely conscious of. In the lengthy notebook devoted
to sleep and dream (only one of "a magnificent number of subjects"
that he took on), he writes of the dreamer: "He will never think. He
will simply be" (*Cahiers* 3:441). This has something to do with what
usually qualifies as thinking, carried on by a disciplined "suppression or repression of the attempt to go beyond" (427). Agatha knows
this, and knows that she is still under the influence of the waking
modes of thought: "Whenever I think to unite, in the midst of the
tenebrous region, ideas that I still possess in their distinctness, I recall that I may well corrupt all the evidence, darkening what I will,
and not necessarily lightening what I will" (209). To the degree that
she is still under this influence, she is held at the borders of sleep,
as reflected in her language: she is "suspended between"; she inhabits an "intervening space"; she is "edged for a few moments around
the same thought." The two following pages describe an intensifying
urge toward an ultimate thought,

something brief, universal: an abstract, imminent pearl would roll
into a deep fold of common thought: an astonishing law, consub-

stantial with its seeker, would inhabit there: work of a moment to get this pearl free: a few words would fix it forever. (210)

Yet this definitive state eludes her; here too we find the language of liminality: she is, she says, "invaded by the residual music of my mind"; the great idea is "always in the tail of the eye"; she is "on the verge of laws . . . trailing a latency." The ultimate thought is an emotion, a desire, that is unattainable and indeed should be so.[17] For "once seen, it would ingest into its own splendid immutability every thought capable of pursuing it; so that the powers of new invention would grow enfeebled" (210). The sense of an imminent great idea, then, is just that: a sense. It arises out of the full presence of the thought or image that presents itself to the mind when it relinquishes "the constant *choice* which characterizes waking." Yet if the nocturnal moment is fully present to one approaching sleep, it is not for that reason immutable: it unfolds and develops in a constant new invention. So, in a residue of waking choice, Agatha acquiesces to this state in which a sense of limpid, pure thoughts coexists with their continual modulation: "Still I preserve the variety of my unease: I maintain a disorder within me the better to attract my own powers or whatever dispersion awaits them" (211).

This "whatever dispersion" is characteristic of Agatha's state now:

> The assemblage of diverse modes of knowing, all equally in prospect, by which I am constituted . . . now forms a system quite null and indifferent to what it might produce or fathom. . . .
>
> An idea rises of itself and takes the place of another: none among them can be more important than its hour.
>
> They ascend, original; in a meaningless order; mysteriously moved toward the admirable noon of my presence, where burns, as it best may, the sole thing that exists: the any *one [l'une quelconque].* (211–12)

There is in Valéry's *quelconque* an odd anticipation of Giorgio Agamben's *qualunque* (in *The Coming Community*), translated, felicitously or not, as "whatever." Perhaps there is no better term to render the difficult notion of a being conceived of as neither generic nor individual: a being that is a singular existence in the world without being understood as a unique collection of traits (woman, communist, artist, Chinese, elderly) or as an abstract generality such as "a person," which is, after all, only another classificatory category. We are coming to grips here with what might be called a zero degree of existence, an existence preceding either the world's categories or those that one determines for oneself in order to determine a self. Such categories, general or particular, fall away with the onset of sleep, along with the rest of "the diverse modes of knowing . . . by which I am constituted." This leaves only the "admirable noon of my presence," burning in the midst of night, a presence that is without distinctness and without distinctions. It is also without choice and the prevailing (though hidden) systems that determine choice; and so it is indifferent to what may or may not be produced by its incessant movement. There is more than a little resemblance between this "whatever" and that realm of perfect indifference and unremitting restlessness evoked by Blanchot as the underworld visited by the Orphean writer.

Significantly, Agamben describes the "whatever" as a liminal or threshold state:

> Whatever adds to singularity only an emptiness, only a threshold: Whatever is a singularity plus an empty space, a singularity that is *finite* and, nonetheless, indeterminable according to a concept. (67)

But if there is only an emptiness beyond the finite singularity of the "whatever," we would seem to be dealing not with a threshold, which is after all an intermediate zone between two states. Rather, this sounds like a *limit*: something beyond which the finite entity cannot pass, as there is nothing into which it could pass. Agamben addresses this problem as follows: "The threshold is not . . . another thing with respect to the limit; it is, so to speak, the experience of the limit itself, the experience of being-*within* an *outside*" (68). This paradoxical state is the one being described by Valéry at this point in *Agatha*. The restless succession of ideas has brought his protagonist to a point where those ideas are, in Agamben's words, "indeterminable according to a concept." And that is the point of Valéry's *l'une quelconque*, and of Agamben's "whatever":

> Whatever is the figure of pure singularity. Whatever singularity has
> no identity, it is not determinate with respect to a concept, but nei-
> ther is it simply indeterminate; rather it is determined only through
> its relation to an *idea*, that is, to the totality of its possibilities. . . .
> It belongs to a whole, but without this belonging's being able to be
> represented by a real condition: Belonging, being-*such*, is here only
> the relation to an empty and indeterminate totality. (67)

The emptiness that has been causing problems here is then the emptiness of the indeterminate, that which is "indeterminable according
to a concept." In Valéry's terms, it is the loss of all the "diverse modes
of knowing . . . by which I am constituted" and thus a real emptying
out. And yet there burns *l'une quelconque*—which nevertheless is not
solitary. In the last words of *Agatha*, of the unfinished *Agatha*, it is
une d'entre elles. *Elles* refers to the ideas that ascend without order,
without ceasing. They ascend toward the "whatever" as the totality
of its possibilities, a totality that can never reach summation. This
final moment of Valéry's work is then simultaneously a threshold
and a limit. It is a threshold in Agamben's sense, in that Agatha is
now inhabiting a zone beyond anything that could be thought of as
her determinate self. But it is also a limit, as she tips over into the
emptiness of sleep. Later in the night she will dream, no doubt; and
Valéry repeatedly and rigorously attempted to understand the nature
of that dream experience.[18] But first she must pass through a zone of
sleep that, if it is a threshold for her, is for Valéry an impassable limit.

TWO

Sleepless

The drop of ink belonging to the sublime night . . .
—STÉPHANE MALLARMÉ

If the process of falling asleep reveals some of the more elusive
processes of consciousness, the same can be said of *not* falling asleep.
By this I do not of course mean being awake as such, but being awake
when one ought to be asleep: insomnia. Insomnia is not, however, a
simple matter of a switch being on when it ought to be off, as indicated by the oddly contradictory history of the word. Basically, it derives
from the Latin *in-* (not) plus *somnus* (sleep). But the second-century
dream interpreter Artemidorus of Daldis applied *insomnia* to a type
of dream, a move that was followed by the fourth-century Macrobius
in his commentary on the *Somnium Scipionis*. There, *insomnia* refers
to dreams that have no divine or prophetic element but arise out of
a sleeper's worries. Nothing helpful or meaningful is to be gained
from these dreams; all they do is disturb the dreamer (Michels 144).
What we retain in English from this contradictory history, according to Eluned Summers-Bremmer, is "the sense of inconstancy, of
wavering on a border—for us, between waking and sleep" (18). Yet if
this sense of the liminal has been retained from insomnia's history,

she goes on to say, something else has been lost: "For the ancients, *insomnia* are dark, desirous dreams within other dark states: sleep, night and death, the deepest. The imbrication of light with agency in the contemporary West makes it difficult to conceive and speak clearly of kinds of darkness that interact with each other in this way" (18). We shall begin with darkness, then, and not without good reason; for the insomniac's experience is first of all and fundamentally an experience of . . .

NIGHT

How can we speak of the night, how can we begin to think it?

The sun sinks, taking with it the light; and this is the moment when, we say, night falls. A curious phrasing: day "breaks," breaks open, a movement that expands outward, but night "falls," falls over the edge of day like a curtain descending. At the same time, its movement is inward: not because it is following the dwindling spark of sun at the horizon, but because darkness is itself an interminable movement inward, the collapse of day's dimensioned objects. For night is first of all an absence, absence of light, and light is what gives shape to the things of the world, structure, the clarity of their distances from each other and their relationships in space. And so night, Maurice Merleau-Ponty argues in *Phenomenology of Perception*, has consequences for both the things of the world and those who observe them:

> Night is not an object before me; it enwraps me and infiltrates through all my senses, stifling my recollections and almost destroying my personal identity. I am no longer withdrawn into my perceptual look-out from which I watch the outlines of objects moving by at a distance. Night has no outlines; . . . it is pure depth without foreground or background, without surfaces and without any distance separating it from me. All space for the reflecting mind is sustained by thinking which relates its parts to each other, but in this case the thinking starts from nowhere. (283)

Two years later, in 1947, Levinas takes up this argument in *Existence and Existents*. Light is what allows the world to be ordered, he asserts;

it "makes possible . . . [an] enveloping of the exterior by the inward, which is the very structure of the cogito, and of sense" (41). So light provides a panoply of metaphors for the ordering activity of the mind, for thought itself: I see your point, it is clear, it is illuminating, brilliant even, you are a bright boy. Night takes all this illumination away along with the shapes of objects, the defined spaces in which both they and their observer are positioned. If the *order* of thought is now dissipated in a nocturnal "nowhere," the same can be said of its *origin*, the place from which it starts: thinking cannot be said to "start" at all, simply because it is revealed as always already in progress. This is thought, of course, that cannot be said to be structured in Levinas's sense, or indeed *as* sense. It is a restless, interminable movement of the mind that reveals itself to us in the night. It does not "get anywhere" any more than it comes from anywhere; it is without goal, defies control, makes no progress while always progressing.

For the "nowhere" of the night is not nothing—which might in its own way bring rest, the nirvana striven for in meditative practice. As Levinas describes it, night brings with it something altogether more disconcerting:

> There is a nocturnal space, but it is no longer empty space, the transparency which both separates us from things and gives us access to them, by which they are given. Darkness fills it like a content; it is full, but full of the nothingness of everything. Can one speak of its continuity? It is surely uninterrupted. But the points of nocturnal space do not refer to each other as in illuminated space; there is no perspective, they are not situated. There is a swarming of points. (53)

With this last sentence Levinas moves, briefly, from the metaphysical to the physical. The phenomenon to which he is referring was described by the Czech scientist Jan Evangelista Purkyně as early as 1819. Purkyně described how, on entering a darkened room, one can "see" numerous small points of moving light, which he compared to the swirling of dust particles in a sunbeam (Wade and Brozek 81). This is one of the effects that can be generated by a *Ganzfeld,* a homogeneous undifferentiated field of vision; a uniformly cloudy sky is another example. At its extreme, a *Ganzfeld* can produce full-blown hallucinations. The suggestion that these hallucinations can be related to hypnagogic images has been raised, only to be disproven through comparisons of EEG records of both phenomena (Wackermann, Pütz, and Allefeld 1370). The swarming points of light, then, are self-reflective manifestations of the eye's activity, as it seeks to see *something*.[1] Levinas is using this phenomenon as the counterpart of another restless motion, that of the mind cast free from its moorings in the daylight world.

To be "cast free" in this sense is not liberating but disorienting: losing situatedness, one loses self. In the dark there is no boundary, there is no center, there is no way to connect the swarm of points, whether spatial or mental. What there is, is "there is"—the *il y a*, as Levinas calls it—the impersonal fact of existence without regard to a coherent existent, the awareness of Being detached from one's own particular being. And this awareness is something like a waking nightmare: "Being is essentially alien and strikes against us. We undergo its suffocating embrace like the night, but it does not respond to us" (9). If it is essentially alien, then Being is other than us, even if it is through participation in Being that our own being comes to be. To say we participate in Being is only to say that we exist—not that we are equivalent to existence, which is something beyond our particular version of it. In the formlessness of night, we experience something of what it is like to be without a self, and yet to sense the pervasive presence of existence.

This is the experience of what Maurice Blanchot calls "the other night"—other in a number of ways. To begin with, this night is other than the day's conception of it, where night is a time of rest and recuperation, "downtime" that is seconded for the day's purposes. Moreover, Blanchot's night is other than the physical fact of darkness—even though darkness, as we have seen, has psychological and philosophical consequences. These consequences, finally, are where the otherness of the "other night" manifests itself. As Blanchot says, "There is no exact moment at which one would pass from night to the *other* night, no limit at which to stop and come back in the other direction" (*Space* 169). Yet perhaps these notions of passing and limitlessness are the most disconcerting characteristics of the other night, where, he says, "the incessant and the uninterrupted reign" (119). Motion without end and existence without form are what one senses in the other night: "Here the invisible is what one cannot cease to see; it is the incessant making itself seen" (163). This may recall Levinas's "swarming of points"—and not surprisingly, given the fact that Levinas and Blanchot repeatedly cross-reference each other on this matter of what happens in the night. Along with the incessant movement of the invisible are other forms of the night's restlessness: "In the night, silence is speech, and there is no repose, for there is no position" (119).

If there is no position, there is also no sleep; for Levinas and Blanchot both view sleep as fundamentally associated with a security of position. Levinas:

> In lying down, in curling up in a corner to sleep, we abandon our-selves to a place; qua base it becomes our refuge. Then all our work of being consists in resting. Sleep is like entering into contact with the protective forces of a place. (67)

Blanchot:

> Where I sleep I fix myself and I fix the world. My person is there, prevented from erring, no longer unstable, scattered and distracted, but concentrated in the narrowness of this place. (*Space* 266)

It is this concentration that we seek when we toss and turn in bed, unable to find exactly the right place that will put a stop to our rest-lessness. "Tossing and Turning," a poem by John Updike, conveys something of the strangeness of this physical restlessness, and the even greater strangeness of its resolution:

> The spirit has infinite facets, but the body
> confiningly few sides.
> There is the left,
> the right, the back, the belly, and tempting
> in-betweens, northeasts and northwests,
> that tip the heart and soon pinch circulation
> in one or another arm.
> Yet we turn each time

with fresh hope, believing that sleep
will visit us here, descending like an angel
          down the angle our flesh's sextant sets,
tilted toward that unreachable star
hung in the night between our eyebrows, whence
dreams and good luck flow.
                Uncross
your ankles. Unclench your philosophy.
This bed was invented by others; know we go
to sleep less to rest than to participate
in the twists of another world.
This churning is our journey.
             It ends,
can only end, around a corner
we do not know
        we are turning.

The poem's last part is ambiguous, and consequently suggests more than it says. Updike dismisses the bed as an invention for rest in much the same way that Blanchot dismisses the idea of night as serving the purposes of the day: the notion that we sleep in order to recuperate our energies for the day's work, and that the bed is the place where we rest. But in contrast to this secure cradle of place, the other night is nonplace: continual distancing, restless movement (in any number of versions) within the incessant, impersonal time that is existence when it is not structured as "our" existence. Is the poem's "another world," then, that of the "other night"? Or is it the world of dream? But these, for Blanchot, are fundamentally akin: "The dream is closer than sleep to the nocturnal region. . . . It is the uninterrupted and the incessant. . . . The dream is the reawakening of the interminable" within sleep (*Space* 267). And the interminable, the incessant, the uninterrupted is also what makes up "our journey" as beings within Being. This is the restless revelation that comes to us in the other night, when we have either left our daylight concerns behind or (more likely) are inundated with them in versions beyond our control: interminable, incessant, uninterrupted. The horror of such moments is that they transform whatever comfort daylight's meaningful agendas may bring to us into a meaningless chatter, repeated endlessly, movement without resolution. There is the suspicion as well that this is the real nature of our existence, which day tries to cover over. When Updike, then, writes, "This churning is our journey," he is not talking just about the tossing and turning of the insomniac; he is talking about the restlessness, the incessant onward drive of our lives to find a stability of self that must always elude us, precisely because of existence's incessant onward drive. There is no way out—except death, the brother of sleep. But that is "a corner we do not know we are turning." This final ironic trope, or turn—to the poem, to the restless turning described within it—is to be read in two ways. It can describe the onset of sleep, the angel of sleep which Kiš's narrator finds impossible to catch in the act. However, it can equally well describe the moment of one's death. I have noted earlier Blanchot's argument that death can never be experienced as such, since the consciousness needed to have an experience is experiencing the extinction of that very consciousness. Thus "we do not know" the moment of our death any more than we know the moment when we cross over into sleep. And perhaps neither of these delivers a way out, since the moment itself is described as a "turning," a continuation of restlessness, with no sense of what lies beyond that turning. "Ay, there's the rub," Hamlet declares,

> For in that sleep of death what dreams may come
> When we have shuffled off this mortal coil
> Must give us pause. (3.1.68–70)

Neither in sleep nor in death is there any guarantee that we will rest in peace.

THE INSOMNIAC WRITER

The desire for sleep, then, is not only a desire for rest so that we can "recharge our batteries" for the day's work; it is also the desire for a respite from existence itself, from its incessant, unrelenting movement. Gerard Manley Hopkins, in his Sonnet 41, finds a meager comfort in the thought that "all / Life death does end and each day dies in sleep." If this is what we hope to find in sleep, though, it is a hope that is continually disappointed. For when we leave our waking state and enter into sleep, it is only to emerge on the other side into that restless waking within sleep that is the dream: "Sleep grows sleepless in dreams," Blanchot writes ("Dreaming, Writing" xxviii). So it is that when "by means of sleep, day uses night to blot out the night" (*Space* 264), this is a strategy that must inevitably fail. Sleep is a delusory escape from the restless essence that is "the other night," a night that is within us as well as without. Yet this is a delusion we willingly accept, that we invite into our beds. And when that invitation is declined, we suffer all the horrors—and sometimes pleasures—of insomnia.

Writers seem to be particularly prone to this nocturnal suffering. It has been suggested that a tendency to insomnia is the trait that, above all others, unites writers of all types and all historical periods (Johnson 643).[2] Naturally the experience of insomnia makes its way into the work of such writers, and from there into anthologies designed to comfort the sleepless by providing words for an experience that may be in the end beyond words.[3] But the writer's relationship to insomnia goes beyond that of the readers of these anthologies, beyond such common causes as an inability to relinquish the concerns of the day or a subliminal fear of death; insomnia becomes the very source of writing. "My trouble is insomnia," Céline declares. "If I had always slept properly, I'd have never written a line" (39). E. M. Cioran—a "career insomniac" according to Willis Regier— said, "I have never been able to write except in the melancholy of insomniac nights" (Regier 994). And Kafka once told his friend Gustav Janouch, "If it were not for these horrible sleepless nights I would never write at all" (Janouch 14). How, then, are we to understand this strangely intimate relation between insomnia and writing?

It should first be made clear that by "insomnia" we are not talking about an occasional difficulty in getting to sleep but rather a relentless, unremitting sleeplessness. Perhaps one might even assert that being "awake" for much of the night is different from being "sleepless"—and this is not a matter of quantity, of counting the hours, but of a fundamental qualitative difference. It is a difference that Hermann Broch stresses at one point in his novel *The Sleepwalkers*:

The sleepless man keeps his eyes closed, as though not to see the cold tomblike darkness in which he lies, not to see it, yet fearing that his sleeplessness may topple over into mere ordinary wakefulness at the sight of the curtains which hang like women's skirts before the window, and all the objects which may detach themselves from the darkness if he were to open his eyes. For he wants to be sleepless and not awake. (313)

Passing over for the moment this curious *desire* to be sleepless, we should first pick up on the implications of that "mere ordinary wakefulness." This is a wakefulness, it seems, that we are familiar with, at home with; it belongs not to the night but to the day, and the difference between them is crucial. There are, according to Cioran, "two kinds of mind: daylight and nocturnal. They have neither the same method nor the same morality" (*Trouble* 17, quoted in Regier 1004). After the insomniac has fully experienced the revelation of the night, he says a bit later, "the day seems useless, light pernicious, even more oppressive than the darkness" (*Trouble* 31). The night's most profound revelation, then, may be the nature of the day, of what we think of as being awake, of a light that claims to illuminate the world in more senses than one. Joyce Carol Oates, another writer who links her productivity to her insomnia, has stated: "Unable to sleep, one suddenly grasps the profound meaning of *being awake*: a revelation that shades subtly into horror, or into instruction" (xiii). She does not dilate any further on this revelation, or the nature of that instruction, but it may be enough for now to underscore the relation of Oates's "being awake" to Levinas's "existence," which, as we have seen, carries its own subtle horror. In an "Invocation to Insomnia," Cioran gives us a sense of what nocturnal instruction is like:

You made me hear the snore of health, human beings plunged into sonorous oblivion, while my solitude engrossed the surrounding dark and became huger than the night. . . . Each night was like the others, each night was eternal. . . . There is no idea which comforts in the dark, no system which resists those vigils. The analyses of insomnia undo all certainties. . . . One does not see in the dark with impunity, one does not gather its lessons without danger; there are eyes which can no longer learn anything from the sun, and souls afflicted by nights from which they will never recover. (*Decay* 169–70)

This devastating effect comes largely from what it is like to *think* in the night, and to be unable to stop thinking. For Cioran this is a mark of night's superiority over the day: "Daylight is hostile to thoughts, the sun blocks them out; they flourish only in the middle of the night" (*Decay* 147). However, the danger, the affliction, of insomnia has to do with what happens to thoughts in the dark. To lie awake in the "other night," Blanchot warns, "leaves thought outside of any secret, deprives it of all intimacy, and turns it into the body of its absence. For it lays thought bare to the lack of thought" (*Disaster* 52).

This seems, on the face of it, an outright contradiction, resolvable only by second thoughts about "thoughts." Certainly, one often-noted characteristic of insomnia is the inability to shut down the mind, the compulsive and unwished-for proliferation of thoughts that keep one from relaxing into sleep. These have a certain progression, Broch notes: "A sleepless night begins with banal thoughts, somewhat as a juggler displays at first banal and easy feats of skill, before proceeding to the more difficult and thrilling ones" (311). If one's thoughts in the night eventually become "thrilling," that is doubtless because, like the juggler's finale, they contain the greatest element of danger. The juggling of strange and far-flung associations, the bewildering sense of how far one has wandered from a simple beginning, is one part of the insomniac's "difficulty." Difficulty is also, no doubt, presented by the sheer difference of nighttime thinking from that of the day. For in the night one reaches no resting point, no conclusion or illuminated "secret" that is not immediately eroded by the continuing flow of thought; and with all the structures of daylight thinking dissolved in the night, the strangest adumbrations are free to appear. Their strangeness means that they cannot be owned or intimate: we do not think, *it thinks*. This "it" should not be given the wrong kind of weight: it is not a malign usurper but merely the adjunct to an action, as William James puts it in his *Psychology*: "If we could say in English 'it thinks,' as we say 'it rains' or 'it blows,' we should be stating the fact most simply and with the minimum of assumption. As we cannot, we must simply say that *thought goes on*" (224–25).

It goes on willfully in the night, dissolving the cogito and the self with it. Of thought's willfulness Broch has this to say: "To the man who is awake such ideas may seem illogical, but he forgets that he himself exists for the most part in a kind of twilight state, and that only the sleepless man in his overwakefulness thinks with really logical severity" (313). This is not a severity designed to ensure the solidity or correctness of one's observations; quite the contrary. It is a severity of thought that undercuts thought at every turn. And it is this ruthless, restless destruction that Blanchot gestures toward when he writes that insomnia "lays thought bare to the lack of thought."

Such revelations of the night are never to be known either by those whose consciousness is laid to rest in sleep or by those who are experiencing Broch's "mere ordinary wakefulness." For the state of insomnia is a liminal one, uneasily situated between sleeping and waking—though the element of waking here is less a matter of open eyes than it is of that waking within sleep that is dream. All these terms or distinctions blur together in the insomniac experience, and with that goes any possibility of sorting out one's thoughts and perceptions according to daylight categories. Consider this elusive diary entry by Franz Kafka for October 2, 1911:

> Sleepless night. The third in a row. I fall asleep soundly, but after an hour I wake up, as though I had laid my head in the wrong hole. I am completely awake, have the feeling that I have not slept at all or only under a thin skin, have before me anew the labor of falling asleep and feel myself rejected by sleep. And for the rest of the night, until about five, thus it remains, so that indeed I sleep but at the same time vivid dreams keep me awake. I sleep alongside myself, so to speak, while I myself must struggle with dreams. About five the last trace of sleep is exhausted, I just dream, which is more exhausting than wakefulness. In short, I spend the whole night in that state in which a healthy person finds himself for a short time before really falling asleep. When I awaken, all the dreams are gathered about me, but I am careful not to reflect on them. Toward morning I sigh into the pillow, because for this night all hope is gone. (*Diaries* 60)

To linger a bit on the contradictions here: he is "completely awake" and "thus it remains, so that indeed I sleep." But then he cannot have

remained awake, especially since at the same time he is having "vivid dreams"—except that these, he says, "keep me awake." Of course
one can dream with eyes wide open, in daydreams or reveries, but
these are indulged in with the dreamer's consent, and Kafka is clearly
struggling with his nocturnal visions. One may also dream with eyes
shut and still be awake; that is the nature of hypnagogia, which is indeed a "state in which a healthy person finds himself for a short time
before really falling asleep," bringing with it a plethora of involuntary
images. In fact, just after this passage, Kafka describes a disturbing
"apparition" *(Erscheinung)*, a blind girl wearing eyeglasses: one eye
is "milky-gray and bulbous," the other recedes and is "covered by a
lens lying close to it"; the eyeglasses are secured to the girl's face by
a support that pierces the flesh and rests on the cheekbone. But the
image's personal specificity and psychological charge move it away
from hypnagogia (whose images, as we have seen, are generally impersonal) and toward dream: Kafka is able to identify a number of
sources for this image—his mother's eyeglasses, an acquaintance's
daughter—in the manner of Freud, with whose work Kafka was of
course familiar.[4] This supports Kafka's designation of these images
as "vivid dreams."

The dreams that haunt the insomniac Kafka, then, are the prod-
ucts not of sleep but of a psychological night; as Oates has observed,
"We experience Night but are also Night" (xiii). The insomniac becomes aware of an incessant inner turbulence that dreams tap into
but that can also surge forward without the intermediary stage of
sleep. So in another entry (July 21, 1913) Kafka writes, "I cannot sleep.
Only dreams, no sleep" (224). The dreamer, however, is other than
the "I" who cannot sleep, for "I sleep alongside myself." This "other"
continually accompanies one, thinking in a manner quite different
from that of the day, though it does not cease during the day. It is
the very fact that this inner turbulence does not cease, is incessant,
that causes Kafka to write, "I just dream, which is more exhausting
than wakefulness." Dream, as Blanchot has described it, is indeed an
endless restless series of resemblances and associations. If we are not
completely exhausted by our dreams, that is because we follow passively where the dreams lead, accepting without question elements

and episodes that will baffle us in the morning when we try to make sense of our dreams, if only to tell them with something like coherence. At that point, however, we are already looking at them with what Cioran would call a daylight mind in contrast to a nocturnal one. Cioran's " nocturnal mind," of course, is not that of dream, but of insomnia—an insomnia that is stripped of the acquiescence that carries us through our dreams but is at the same time impelled by a kind of dream logic. The collision between these two mental modes is what produces the insomniac's incessant, and incessantly self-destroying, thoughts. For the writer, these can become the errant path of "inspiration," a term to which we will return in a moment. So it is that Kafka repeatedly connects his sleeplessness to his writing— although, appropriately enough, he never decides which precedes the other. In another part of his October 2 diary entry he says:

> I believe this sleeplessness comes only because I write. For no matter how little and how badly I write, I am still made sensitive by these minor shocks, feel, especially toward evening and even more in the morning, the approaching, the imminent possibility of great moments which would tear me open, which could make me capable of anything, and in the general uproar that is within me and which I have no time to command, find no rest. (61)

But if sleeplessness comes with writing, writing also demands sleeplessness. For, as Kafka writes to Felice Bauer (January 15, 1913), "writing means revealing oneself to excess. . . . That is why one can never be alone enough when one writes, why there can never be enough silence around one when one writes, why even night is not night enough" (*Letters* 156). It is not that night provides a "cover" for one's excesses, but that night is the very milieu of excess, of a continual passing beyond limits. The riskiest revelations of the day, Kafka says in the same letter, still fall short of what is required for writing; only the night gives the writer what he needs, and even the "great moments" of the night, as he says, may not be enough.

How does this nocturnal instruction find its way into Kafka's writing? However much he may write of insomnia in diaries or letters, it does not figure in his work, but nevertheless, one senses its

presence. To begin with, it is there in the sheer liminality of his stories, which like their insomniac author lie somewhere between sleeping and waking. Elements that seem dreamlike are presented with
scrupulously realistic detail that resists any such classification as
"dream narrative." This resistance can sometimes be explicit, as it is
in "The Metamorphosis." The story begins as Gregor Samsa awakes
from "uneasy dreams." Waking, as we will see later, is for Kafka always a dangerous transition, and a doubtful one in the sense that we
cannot be entirely sure that the transition has been made completely.
In this case, because of the powerful pull of the dreamlike premise,
the reader may remain unsure, even though Gregor himself quickly
decides, "It was no dream," and even though the dreamlike premise
is developed in a fully detailed realism. Another kind of undecid-
ability characterizes any work by Kafka, and that is the question of
what it "means"—a daylight question, to be sure, and one that in the
work is given a nocturnal answer, which is to say no answer. This "no
answer" is not a simple denial or recalcitrant silence; it is a prolongation, perhaps even a multiplication, of the question. The work gives
rise to what Lois Nesbitt has called "critical insomnia"—by which she
does not mean being kept awake by problematic texts. It is rather a
model of thought, which she both investigates and recommends. The
insomniac, she writes,

> circles around his obsession, viewing it from different perspectives
> and arriving at different interpretations of its significance. The pro-
> cess is infinite: the insomniac may return to and reconsider earlier
> interpretations, but he is never able to commit himself to any one
> reading of the facts. His mental journey may reveal characteristics
> of logical thought: fixity of object, systematic analysis of that object,
> linear or sequential enumeration of ideas. But this logic is at best
> temporary; in the long run his path is as irrational as it is rational,
> for the links between one idea and the next are often rather the leaps
> of associative thinking, metonymic slides from one track to another.
> Patterns are generated, but their instigation is contingent upon fac-
> tors both relevant and irrelevant, justifiable and specious.
>
> What distinguishes insomniac thinking from idle contemplation,
> however, is the constancy of its object. One motion leads to another

and another, but the insomniac's path is circular and not linear; his attention remains focused on the center of that circle. (3)

This description of insomniac thinking becomes that of critical thinking, Nesbitt asserts, in the case of "texts whose very structures and textures force us to become insomniac readers" (2).

Kafka's *The Castle* is one such text. If insomniac thought is circular, as Nesbitt suggests, here the center of the circle, the focus of attention, is the castle itself. Not that the focus is clear enough to repay that attention: "There was no sign of the Castle hill, fog and darkness surrounded it, not even the faintest gleam of light suggested the large Castle. K. stood a long time on the wooden bridge that leads from the main road to the village, gazing upward into the seeming emptiness." With these words both K. and Kafka enter the world of the novel, and we enter it with them. The transition to literature, Blanchot intimates while citing this passage, is also the transition *of* literature, its continual doubling not so much of "life" as of every literary work that has preceded the one we are reading, with no ground other than that provided by such a repetition. This sort of transition is also K.'s, since, "in an incomprehensible manner, he decides to break with his own familiarity, as though pulled ahead toward these sites nonetheless without allure by an exigency he is unable to account for. From this perspective," Blanchot concludes, "one would almost be tempted to say that the entire meaning of the book is already borne by the *wooden bridge*," a liminal zone to be sure (*Infinite Conversation* 463n3). When the Castle becomes visible in the next day's light, it first meets K.'s expectations and then disappoints them: "It was only a rather miserable little town, pieced together from village houses, distinctive only because everything was perhaps built of stone, but the paint had long since flaked off, and the stone seemed to be crumbling" (8). As with the "seeming emptiness," there is a good deal of the merely ostensible here, and the promise of a meaningful center deteriorates into the messiness of ordinary life. Similarly, as K. continues to seek the Castle, his focus branches out into numerous digressions, reversals, and blind alleys—a psychology that is expressed by a certain topography. "The vicious circularity of Kafka's spaces has often been noted," Dorrit Cohn writes (22), and goes on to quote from the beginning of the novel:

> So he set off again, but it was a long way. The street he had taken, the main street in the village, did not lead to the Castle hill, it only went close by, then veered off as if on purpose, and though it didn't lead any farther from the Castle, it didn't get any closer either. K. kept expecting the street to turn at last toward the Castle and it was only in this expectation that he kept going.[5]

This literalizes Nesbitt's notion of "the insomniac's path"; but of course the topography here reflects a certain movement of thought.

Blanchot has described that movement in rather different terms: "In the night," he says, "insomnia is dis-cussion: not the work of arguments bumping against other arguments, but the extreme shuddering of no thoughts, percussive stillness (the exegeses that come and go in *The Castle,* story of insomnia)" (*Disaster* 49). *The Castle,* like many other works of Kafka, does indeed include endless discussion: speculations, explanations, interpretations. These are often at odds with one another and reverse themselves even as they are being put forward—as does the reasoning of the animal in "The Burrow," who seeks to secure another version of the Castle, his "Castle Keep." Blanchot expresses this movement through an ingenious deconstructive etymology, breaking *discussion* in two (the word is the same in French and English). The last half, *-cussion,* is related to the "bumping" that is more clearly evident in words such as *concussion* and *percussion*; it is ultimately derived from the Latin *quatere,* to shake. The negating prefix *dis* turns conflicting thoughts into nothoughts, a turn that they make all too readily in the insomniac state. The more the insomniac pursues problems in the night, the more they lead inevitably to a final dis-solution, which is not a resting point but, rather, "percussive stillness."

Another word for this "percussive stillness" might be *rustling,* which at first glance seems to belong to an entirely different audial order; but the psychological order expressed through these sounds is of a piece. We return to Levinas, who in *Existence and Existents* at several points refers to a "rustling" that he links to the *there is (il y a).*

"The rustling of the *there is* . . . is horror," he declares (55), and specifies the nature of that horror on the following page:

> In horror a subject is stripped of his subjectivity, of his power to have private existence. The subject is depersonalized. . . . It is a participation in the *there is* which returns in the heart of every negation, in the *there is* that has "no exits." (56)

The horror is evoked, then, by the sense of "pure" existence—something that is beyond one's "own" particular existence. As Levinas later puts it, "Identity is something that belongs not to the verb *to be,* but to . . . a noun which has detached itself from the anonymous rustling of the *there is*" (88). Existence is an interminable neutral verb: it is the incessant movement of *now* and *now* and *now* and *now,* a continual restatement of being in time, beyond any content or design. This movement may be thought of as itself a kind of rustling, beneath the articulated personal concerns of one's life. Levinas's notion of "rustling" has affinities with that of Roland Barthes:

> The rustle is the noise of what is working well. From which follows this paradox: the rustle denotes a limit-noise, an impossible noise of what, functioning to perfection, has no noise: to rustle is to make audible the very evaporation of noise. ("Rustle" 76–77)

What is working well, only too well, is existence's remorseless persistence. It is like a well-oiled machine, one that we do not control, but rather controls us: "We dread the machine when it works by itself," Barthes observes (76). The rustle is a "limit-noise" because it is close to being no noise at all; yet it underlies the noise of our daily preoccupations, daylight scenarios that evaporate in the night, making audible a horror that was always present. "The impossibility of rending the invading, inevitable, and anonymous rustling of existence" says Levinas, "manifests itself particularly in certain times when sleep evades our appeal" (61).

Yet we may ask whether "the rustle" is wholly distinct from the noise of our daylight agendas, our ongoing articulation of ourselves to ourselves. For after his description of what a rustle is or does, Barthes asks, "And language—can language rustle?" He answers his own question as follows:

Just as, when attributed to the machine, the rustle is only the noise
of an absence of noise, in the same way, shifted to language, it would
be that meaning which reveals an exemption of meaning or—the
same thing—that non-meaning which produces in the distance a
meaning henceforth liberated from all the aggressions of which the
sign, formed in the "sad and fierce history of men," is the Pandora's
box. (77)

Such a liberation is for Barthes a positive good to be deliberately
sought by writers. But sometimes, in the dark hours of the night,
it comes to writers—and others—unsought, unbidden; and at such
times it oppresses them with horror—a horror that is not unrelated
to language. When insomniacs complain of not being able to "turn
off" their minds, the relentless succession of thoughts that they are
subjected to is, as often as not, verbalized: one rants, orates, explains,
remembers even—in words. These are usually words that are only
too familiar: one is "going over the same ground" over and over. This
"over and over" is a repetition that can lead to a familiar effect: the
evacuation of all meaningfulness from the words.[6] Words, that is,
and the only-too-familiar thought patterns that they embody, reveal
themselves to be mere noise. And that noise, to the degree that it is
without meaning, approaches the condition of no-noise, in somewhat
the same way that the rustle, for Barthes, is "the noise of an absence
of noise," or the way that Blanchot's other night "lays thought bare
to the lack of thought" (*Disaster* 52). In both cases, the insomniac
turn of mind turns something into "the body of its absence" (52).
That absence is not mere void, for a void would mean an end to the
insomniac's restlessness. It is a "percussive stillness," to return to
Blanchot's formulation, that merges with the rustle of the *there is*, of
impersonal, reiterative existence. An absence (of meaning in one's
personal thoughts) merges with a presence (of unremitting impersonal existence) until they become interchangeable, indistinguishable. There is horror enough in this nocturnal revelation, and never
more than when one realizes that it applies as well to the day. To
repeat Oates's sentence: "Unable to sleep, one suddenly grasps the
profound meaning of *being awake*: a revelation that shades subtly into
horror, or into instruction" (xiii).

The horror experienced in the night is of course itself a form of instruction, but a writer may learn something more from lying awake in the night: something about the nature of language, or about the power of certain images (like Kafka's waking dreams), or about the implications of insomnia for other states. It is not surprising, then, that insomniac writers feel compelled to write about their insomnia, and to do so in an insomniac mode.

There is no better example of this compulsion than Blake Butler's *Nothing: A Portrait of Insomnia*. Butler, still a young man (thirty-two) at this writing, has been a lifelong insomniac. From infancy he suffered night terrors, and as a child would go to school with dark circles under his eyes. He was once sleepless for an uninterrupted 129 hours. His portrait of insomnia cannot be assigned to any one genre; it calls upon personal memoir, history, scientific study, statistics, and literature, moving among them with a fluidity that reflects the restlessness of insomniac thought. It also includes long passages written in a hallucinatory mode, conveying the disconcerting shift out of familiar reality that is the result of prolonged sleeplessness. For Butler, that familiar reality is the house where he grew up and still has a room. In one episode he finds, by the street outside his house, a wire that he has never seen before, bolted to the ground and leading away "into the nowhere of the night" (214). He follows it. Memories crowd his brain as he moves through the neighborhood, still holding the wire, and the night that has been moonless becomes strangely illuminated:

> Behind my head the moon grows glowing so hot and fast I have to close my lids to keep from burning, and then and there under my lids I hear the moon blink with me—*burning out*—so that there at once in my unseeing the air around the earth also cannot see— the fields and houses and the hours cloaked with nothing around my nothing, a darkness deeper than no mind in mirror cloak— a darkness time could not erase in new directions—ageless black unleaving. I swallow and hear shapes. I rub my finger and my thumb together and feel the words between them screech, wanting out into the dark where they could hide from paper and from thinking— to slip into no light and never be remade—all my words ever only wanting in this in me—to go nowhere. (216)

This "nowhere" is a nocturnal one; the night is both goal and origin of his words. Here as elsewhere in Butler's writing, his language conveys not only the strangeness of the experience but also a strangeness in language itself: he gives us odd formulations such as "a darkness deeper than no mind in mirror cloak." One understands something from this, but it is not a lucid language, a language belonging to the light. Butler is following Dickinson's advice to "tell it slant" (506). This strategy sometimes seems to collapse into malapropism: for instance, child-rearing manuals "beget more attenuation to the child beget the child's increasing attenuation to the self" (82); streetlights are "blurting the smaller stars out" (79). Yet despite these moments, or perhaps even because of them, Butler's language may be the closest literary equivalent we have to the liminal state that is insomnia. We hover between understanding what he is saying and not understanding how he is saying it. If some words can be impostors for other words, all words are impostors for the states of mind they claim to convey. Butler's warping of language varies in intensity depending on what he is conveying: information about scientific research is rendered in something that approaches a daylight style; descriptions of how insomnia *feels* are rendered in night writing. Yet whatever local bewilderments may be folded into his language, its affect is always powerfully evident. Bewilderment indeed permeates the book, which is a passionate casting off from the secure, the familiar, the lucid—into the nowhere of the night, in search of nothing.

Blanchot has reminded us that we can and should distinguish among various versions of nothing: he warns us, for instance, against the nothingness that stands as a dramatic antagonist against which one may define one's existential self, suggesting instead a nothingness that is perfectly indifferent to any such posture. Levinas's "nothing" is different from either of these, a crowded restless entity. The "nothing" of Butler's book title is like Levinas's night: "It is full, but full of the nothingness of everything." Butler connects the insomniac state to—if not "everything"—a range that encompasses the restless proliferations of the Web and his father's descent into dementia. In "The Uncontrollable Reflection," a section that attempts to trace the progress, or rather nonprogress, of an insomniac's thoughts during a sleepless night, Butler evokes a terror reminiscent of Levinas's *il y a*:

And still here I am exactly in this dry and endless furled unfurling when, this when there waiting somewhere just above us and soon coming, always coming, nothing, something soft without a name, its thick face shitting in endless squirm-moves through silent tunnels hidden on the night, ripping hard and roared toward anywhere surrounding with the presence of a hammer to a fontanel, a blood spot in a rover, how any hour any every other could be oncoming and there would mostly be no way to know, no signal shot from silent objects scrying until there they are upon us or within us and still here I am again, again again. (66)

To ask for a more coherent language here would be to ask for more control over a state that is uncontrollable. The terror of the insomniac's night thoughts comes from their multiplying rush, reflected here in a rhythmic writing that pulses with its own desperate power.

And that multiplies still further in the form of footnotes. These often have to do with writing, writing as akin to insomnia. Just as in insomnia "the thought births the next thought," so it is in writing, the footnote tells us: "Each sentence a container for each other sentence" (40). And in later footnotes: "Words bouncing other words out of them in a silence, refracted by association, filling out the flesh around the flesh inside the head with what" (41); "Inside the sentence, each word or image shits another, and from each of those, again, again" (43); "The drift between each instance of any word that much larger than the word itself" (44). The implication is that writing, like insomnia, takes place in a liminal realm between the modes of daylight and night:

This kind of inverse relation, in my own body, often leaves me feeling as if I am more truly awake when I am asleep, and more asleep when I'm awake—opening the question of who in me or through me is doing the writing. (59)

The idea that something in the writer but beyond the writer is doing the writing—this approaches the traditional idea of *inspiration*. Blanchot revisits this hoary notion and revives it in unexpected ways. Inspiration is for him "a nocturnal state" within which the writer lingers "in search of an errant word" (*Space* 182). Errancy itself is the wandering essence of something that has no center and no conclusion, just as it is the essence, or nonessence, of insomnia. Thus Blanchot can write: "Inspiration, that errant word which cannot come to an end, is *the long night of insomnia*" (*Space* 184). And in both inspiration and insomnia there is a dissolution of identity, a going beyond the self that is not willed by the self: "The purer the inspiration," Blanchot writes, "the more dispossessed is he who enters the space where it draws him" (*Space* 182). Dispossessed, among other things, of all possibility for rest: "Inspiration pushes us gently or impetuously out of the world, and in this outside there is no sleep, any more than there is rest" (*Space* 185). While there is a sense in which one writes in order to lay to rest the errant word, to fix it on the page and thus to earn the right to sleep, one who has truly understood the night's lessons will resist this drive to a final and fixed production. The writer's words will continue to be errant, will draw the reader—as the author has been drawn before this—into the restless outside that provided the author's inspiration, and now must provide the reader's. The writer, then, will seek "*to make of the work a road toward inspiration . . . and not of inspiration a road toward the work*" (*Space* 186). The aim of such a work, that is, is to reproduce in the reader the state of mind in which it came to be, to induce a "critical insomnia" even in those who are not critics.

NIGHT WATCH

If the writer's inspiration is in some fundamental way insomniac, it follows that for all the complaining there is yet a *desire* to be sleepless, to reap the rewards of insomnia. Cioran puts it like this:

> True knowledge comes down to vigils in the darkness: the sum of our insomnias alone distinguishes us from the animals and from our kind. What rich or strange idea was ever the work of a sleeper? Is your sleep sound? Are your dreams sweet? You swell the anonymous crowd. (*Decay* 147)

Like many insomniacs, Cioran's pride in sleeplessness is paired with a disdain for those who all too easily wallow in swinish sleep. Vladimir Nabokov is in perfect accord: "Sleep is the most moronic fraternity in the world . . . [a] nightly betrayal of reason, humanity, genius" (*Speak* 108). Genius belongs only to the one who wakes in the night, the night that offers perceptions not accessible to daylight thinking. And so the sleepless hours are denominated "vigils" by Cioran, in a kind of secular sanctification. The vigil of insomnia must, however, be distinguished from vigilance, and is so distinguished by Blanchot:

> Night is foreign to the vigilance which is ever exercised, carried out, and which conveys lucid reason toward what it must maintain in reflection—in the preservation, that is, of its own identity. Wakeful-ness is estrangement: it does not waken, as if emerging from a sleep that would precede it, yet it reawakens: constant and instant return to the immobility of the wake. Something wakes: something keeps watch without lying in wait or spying. The disaster watches. . . . Watching is not the power to keep watch—in the first person; it is not a power, but the touch of the powerless infinite, exposure to the other of the night, where thought renounces the vigor of vigilance. (*Disaster* 48)

Vigil, watch, wake—historically these words are often interchanged; yet we can briefly underscore their different connotations before in-tertwining them again. A *vigil* is associated with something that is to be revered; its watching is a devotional act, like that undertaken before a religious festival or investiture as a knight. Or the watch-ing may be over a body on the night preceding burial: the *wake*. A *watch*, in contrast, is undertaken to guard against a danger; it is un-dertaken for the sake of those who are then secure enough to sleep. Blanchot plays with and against this sense, for in the above passage what watches *is* the danger: "The disaster watches." *The disaster* is of course a complex term in Blanchot, something that can be ges-tured toward, circled around, but not defined in terms acceptable to the daylight mind—for it is precisely that which threatens the day's knowledge. It is a nocturnal revelation of all that is indifferent to human existence, an indifference in which "existence" itself, the *il y a*, partakes. Those who are sleepless may begin by thinking that it is they who are watching the night pass, keeping watch over its rev-elations. But at a certain time—perhaps F. Scott Fitzgerald's "three o'clock in the morning"—they realize that they are not spectators of an unfolding knowledge, but rather that the night is watching them. *"Keep watch over absent meaning"*: this is, in its entirety, one of Blanchot's axioms from *The Writing of the Disaster* (42). It is unclear to whom it is addressed: to himself, to the reader, to the disaster that *is* to a great degree absent meaning? To all of these, perhaps, and to the writer above all. For if the insomniac writer has the terrible privilege of access to a knowledge that is fundamentally other, along with that comes an equally terrible responsibility: to write it.

This is perhaps the real subject of an enigmatic short piece, "At Night," by Kafka:

> Deeply lost in the night. Just as one sometimes lowers one's head to reflect, thus to be utterly lost in the night. All around people are asleep. It's just play acting, an innocent self-deception, that they sleep in houses, in safe beds, under a safe roof, stretched out or curled up on mattresses, in sheets, under blankets; in reality they have flocked together as they had once upon a time and again later in a deserted region, a camp in the open, a countless number of men, an army, a people, under a cold sky on cold earth, collapsed where once they had stood, forehead pressed on the arm, face to the ground, breathing quietly. And you are watching, are one of the watchmen, you find the next one by brandishing a burning stick from the brushwood pile beside you. Why are you watching? Someone must watch, it is said. Someone must be there. (*Stories* 436)

The security that is a precondition of sleep—a security of *place,* as has already been noted—is here dissolved. We have, instead, the vision of a place that is the closest thing to a nonplace: "a deserted region" that is nevertheless filled with "a countless number"; that is to say, there is *only* this countless number in a vaguely denominated "region" that is deserted by everything else—a desert. It is "open"— too open, since there is nothing to close one's gaze and nothing to shield people from exposure to an elemental landscape, cold sky and cold earth. This is Blanchot's "nocturnal region" (*Space* 267), with all that we have seen it to imply. The sleepers that we find here are not comfortably resting in order to recoup their energies for the following day: they have collapsed. If they are an "army," they are in extre-

mis, worn out by their battles. Their unnamed antagonist may well
be the night itself, in which they are "deeply lost"—as are we, at the
piece's opening, for it is not specified who is lost. A comparison that
implicitly claims to clarify things only obscures them further: "Just
as one sometimes lowers one's head to reflect, thus to be utterly lost
in the night." The sentence's structure is askew, for the comparison
is not about lowering the head but about reflection. And when we
understand this, we have still not understood; for how is reflection,
with its connotations of conscious and responsible thinking, like being lost in the night? Only, perhaps, in the way that thoughts, when
pursued far enough, become nonthoughts, branch out into an interminable region where we find no secure home. This homelessness is
our primal condition, which we try to cover over by fixing ourselves
in various ways: within actual houses, within constructed identities,
within structured systems of ideas. Uncovering all this as "an innocent self-deception," Kafka expresses the state that underlies this
deception through a vaguely delineated primitivism.

And here too there is a "watch" within the night. It seems at
first that this is a watch undertaken to keep danger away, in order that the sleepers may remain secure. But of course it is never
Kafka's project to reassure us of our security, to shore up that
self-deception, however innocent it may be. The question is still
open—"Why are you watching?"—and the answer retreats into
an unknown authority: "Someone must watch, it is said." Yet by
whom it is said is not specified. The impersonality of "it is said"
carries over into the last sentence: "Someone must be there."
Since no reason is given for being there, the force of "must" may
apply to the being there itself: a version, perhaps, of Levinas's
il y a. A state of pure existence demands that one sense its remorse-
lessness—unless one subscribes to that innocent self-deception, as
most of us do, bowing to an equally urgent "must." Only in the watches of the night, when anodyne sleep has failed us, do we glimpse
something of the impersonal existence that bears up what we like
to think of as "our" existence. This nocturnal revelation comes notably to the writer—or writers, since the speaker here is only one of a
number of watchmen, scattered at distant intervals in the dark. For

Kafka, his fellow watchmen would have been authors such as Hugo von Hofmannsthal or Robert Walser. Their lights are few and far between, and are unheeded by the sleepers. There is a sense of compassion for these oblivious ones, and yet one cannot watch *over* them—one can only watch. And to the degree that one's *being there* is not one's own, this statement too must be corrected. Levinas writes: "It is not that there is *my* vigilance in the night; in insomnia it is the night itself that watches. It watches" (63). But that watching may speak, however strangely, through the writer's words. After all, Kafka tells us that someone, rather than something, watches. That someone is the writer, the insomniac of inspiration, the subject become anonymous object of the other night.

THREE

Leaving Sleep

When the call to "wake up!" is sounded by anything from a revolutionary movement to a letter to the editor, the benefits of being awake are commonly contrasted to the sodden torpor of sleep. It is of course invariably an outside observer who issues the wake-up call, and from that vantage point the usual similarities between sleep and death are evident enough. But if the one who is sleeping is also dreaming, no such torpor exists. If anything, the sleeper's experience may be more rapid and highly charged than the plodding and repetitive patterns that make up most of daily life. So a significant shift in our understanding occurs when we experience sleep, as it were, from the inside. And another shift in our understanding occurs when we approach the moment of waking in the same way. We wake up every day, and yet it can be argued that we almost never experience that curious transition from the inside. There are too many pressures from the outside hustling us rapidly, too rapidly, from one side of this threshold to another: the brutal sounding of the alarm clock, the psychological imperative to get up and get on with it. If for a moment we experience a dazed sense of peculiarity, that very dazedness will help ensure that we won't think for very long about just what it is that makes waking peculiar: who can philosophize first thing in the morning? Our habitual patterns and perceptions—of waking among other things—close ranks; we stumble out of bed and take our place in those ranks. Perhaps it is only when waking takes a peculiar form that we get a sense of how peculiar it has been all along. We understand rightly what is at stake here only when we wake up wrong.

WAKING UP AWRY

To better understand the transition that is waking, then, we can begin by looking at one of the best-known literary descriptions of waking up wrong: it is that moment, near the beginning of *Swann's Way,* when Marcel emerges from sleep into a darkened room. The passage first describes an ordinary, unproblematic transition from sleeping to waking. "A sleeping man," we are told, "holds in a circle around him the sequence of the hours, the order of the years and worlds. He consults them instinctively as he wakes and reads in a second the point on the earth he occupies, the time that has elapsed before his waking; but their ranks can be mixed up, broken" (5) by various unusual circumstances. Or not so unusual. "It was enough," Marcel says, "if, in my own bed, my sleep was deep and allowed my mind to relax entirely; then it would let go of the map of the place where I had fallen asleep and, when I woke in the middle of the night, since I did not know where I was, I did not even understand in the first moment who I was" (5). Rapidly he runs through a number of possibilities, trying to orient himself by imposing on the unresponsive darkness the contours and contents of the various bedrooms he has inhabited during his life. Dimly sensed objects become place markers, markers of place and thus of the time in which those places are inhabited. Without any objects at all there would be no place; and place, as has frequently been argued, is as important to Proust's project as is time. For it is the specific details and the atmosphere of a place that give the moment the distinctive character that constitutes it as a discernible entity in time. So it is that Marcel can make the startling transition "since I did not know where I was, I did not even understand . . . who I was." His disorientation is at the same time topographical, chronological, and ontological. The circle of hours, years, and worlds that encompasses the sleeper now becomes no longer a reassuring and stable containment but a dizzying disorientation. The compass remains stable perhaps, but the needle is spinning wildly: "When I woke thus," Marcel tells us, "everything revolved around me in the darkness, things, countries, years . . . [even if] these revolving, confused evocations never lasted for more than a few seconds" (6–7). They are, however, significant seconds.

In this passage, the sense of place is ruptured at the moment when sleep is ruptured, sleep that is in certain ways bound up with place, as we have seen earlier. "Sleep," Levinas writes in *Existence and Existents*, "is like entering into contact with the protective forces of a place; to seek after sleep is to gropingly seek after that contact. When one wakes up one finds oneself shut up in one's immobility like an egg in its shell" (70).[1] This is physically true, but psychologically— as the passage from Proust has demonstrated—things may be quite otherwise, the very antithesis of the protected and the secure. Here, for instance, is a chilling passage from David Wojnarowicz's memoir *Close to the Knives*:

> This morning I woke up in another part of my brain. . . . When I opened my eyes, I woke with a feeling of confusion and a sense that something indiscernible had shifted during the sleeping hours and now I was somewhere else, not in another place physically, but something similar. The "I" of *my self* had crawled through the thickness of memory and consciousness to some other plane in the structure of the brain and emerged within a new gray coil. When my eyes opened, I felt I was viewing the once familiar room through a four-foot thick piece of slightly yellowed glass. . . . I fought the urge to lay down and return to sleep in order to regain my proper place, to shift back into a developing place where for thirty-odd years I'd been waking up. (61)

Franz Kafka also knew something about the perils of waking, as explicated in an excised passage of *The Trial*:

As someone said to me–I can't remember now who it was—it is really remarkable that when you wake up in the morning you nearly always find everything in exactly the same place as the evening before. For when asleep and dreaming you are, apparently at least, in an essentially different state from that of wakefulness; and therefore, as that man truly said, it requires enormous presence of mind, or rather quickness of wit, when opening your eyes to seize hold as it were of everything in the room at exactly the same place where you had let it go on the previous evening. That was why, he said, the moment of waking up was the riskiest moment of the day. Once that was well over without deflecting you from your orbit, you could take heart of grace for the rest of the day. To which conclusion that man—I have incidentally remembered now who it was, but the name is unimportant . . . (257–58)[2]

Kafka's coyness here about the identity of the man—not remembering, then remembering, then deciding it is unimportant to remember—is a playful reference to his best friend, Max Brod. Along with another of Kafka's friends, Felix Weltsch, Brod had authored a philosophical study, *Anschauung und Begriff*. At its core is the formula $(A + x)$, where A is a general base of similar phenomena and x is a differing and distinct one; together these are seen to account for the processes cited in the title: perception and thought. Joel Morris has summed up the argument of the book, which Kafka found tedious to get through because of its abstractness. One specific example, however, seems to have stuck with him:

It can indeed happen that in your own bed you do not know yourself when at night you suddenly emerge from sleep—that in your own room, right and left, you are confused by a strange feeling and can form no representation of the furniture's accustomed arrangement. Until here too the $(A + x)$ images wake and in a single stroke organize everything in the familiar way! (Morris 479; translation mine)

No doubt Kafka's observation was in Blanchot's mind when he wrote, "To be surprised at finding everything still there in the morning is to forget that nothing is surer than sleep" (*Space* 266). However, Blanchot also seems to have forgotten something, if only momentarily: that within the security of sleep is something that is in many ways its direct opposite. That something, of course, is the dream. And if in sleep we secure ourselves in rest, in dream we open into a restlessness without end. Here is how Blanchot describes this restless movement:

> The dream touches the region where pure resemblance reigns. Everything there is similar: each figure is another one, is similar to another and to yet another, and this last to still another. One seeks the original model, wanting to be referred to a point of departure, an initial revelation, but there is none. The dream is the likeness that refers eternally to likeness. (*Space* 268)[3]

The contrast between Kafka's fascination with returning to the "same place" at the moment of waking and Blanchot's interminable series of similitudes is, for Heidegger, the basic contrast between waking and dreaming. He writes to his friend Medard Boss:

> Waking up consists precisely in [the fact] that one encounters the world as the same one he is accustomed to in being awake. The waking world is characterized by the identical enduring of things, of other human beings, and of how they move about in it. . . . While dreaming, one does not encounter the same, but . . . what is alike. (228)

Sameness versus similitude. And because sameness is an "identical enduring," it can be related to *place*, while the similitudes of dreams interminably displace themselves within an internal *space*.

The philosopher Thorsten Botz-Bornstein, in an essay on the space of dream, has stated that in dream "we do not meet beings (which are what they are) because here . . . Being is always different from the place in which it exists" (174). This differing from place is also a differing that is inherent in resemblance, which is distinguished from identity precisely by the element of difference. Thus we get the pronouncement of John Shade in Nabokov's *Pale Fire*: "Resemblances are the shadows of differences" (265). The continual differing of resemblances is the very antithesis of the consolidating, the concentration, that is place. If I describe that antithesis as "space," there is a danger that space may be conceived of as merely a larger version of place, a static extension within which things appear.

The alternative to this common conception of space, Botz-Bornstein suggests, is "a reality in which time and space form a playful unity that is perceived *through imagination* by the human mind" (177). The playfulness here can be linked both to Derridean play and to Blanchot's interminable play of resemblances. If sleep is a place where the self, centered in a body, settles into a site, dream in Blanchot's view lacks a center, is always eccentric ("Dreaming, Writing" xxiv), and is always in motion. It could be described as "an infinite theatre of movement"—Henri Bergson's phrase for space. Within the space of dream there is a continual play of movement—only what is at play is not things but images. So I choose to read Botz-Bornstein's perhaps unfortunate reference to the human imagination in terms of *image,* rather as Blanchot does in his essay "The Two Versions of the Imaginary," where the imaginary is simply that which pertains to the image. It is significant that the complex terms in which he reads the image in that essay are bound up with notions of distance and the interminable, an interminable distance that is not unrelated to the way I am describing space. Thus "to live an event as an image" resembles what it is like to dream. It is, in Blanchot's words, "to pass from the region of the real where we hold ourselves at a distance from things the better to order and use them into that other region where the distance holds us—the distance which then is the lifeless deep, an unmanageable, inappreciable remoteness which has become something like the sovereign power behind all things. This movement implies infinite degrees" (*Space* 261). The antithesis of place, this is a continual movement *away* from the centered self and, indeed, in its "infinite degrees," from that movement itself. Yet this is not to say that this interminable movement is alien to the dreamer. Rather, we may apply to the space of dream what Blanchot says of image: "The image is intimate. For it makes of our intimacy an exterior power which we suffer passively. Outside of us . . . there trails, like glistening debris, the utmost depth of our passions" (*Space* 262).

The utmost depth of our passions may at times seem rather shallow; the really extraordinary dreams (at least so far as we remember them) are few and far between. Which of us has not gratefully subsided into sleep after a day of boring and repetitive activity, only to find that our dreams continue this activity in almost exactly the same terms? Yet that "almost" alerts us to a resemblance that is also a difference. No matter how domestic or domesticated our concerns in the dream may be, the *mode* in which they are experienced is otherwise than in our conscious waking moments. At times the play of dreams skates over the surface, like Yeats's long-legged fly; but in its very play, its always sensed potential for transformation, it opens to us a space of mobility that is *essentially* different from the place that we occupy in waking life.

It is time to return to that place, and to the moment of waking. I have described the space of dream as one of play, and in doing so have put into play a number of concepts that have their various resemblances and differences. My associative method, that is, has been somewhat dreamlike—as the play of thought may often be. I cannot hope within this network of notions to have captured the "dream-sensation" (as Marlow calls it in *Heart of Darkness*), but only to have gestured toward it. Yet this gesture may be enough to justify my assertion now that the moment of waking is always a moment of loss. We are not displaced from dream so much as placed, returned to the condition of place; for at that moment the spaciousness of dream, its infinite filamentation within a mental space, is suddenly contracted. The containedness of place that both Levinas and Blanchot saw as an asset to sleep, a security within which one can let one's self rest, can also be seen as a limitedness. We awake into a body that is indeed the definitive place, a continuous "here" that we can never transform into a "there." It is the condition of our fated placement in the world— fated because we do not choose this place, which is not like any other because it *is us*. It is the incarnation of Heidegger's notion of "thrownness": we are thrown into the body, into the world, into time. And this primordial fatality is repeated every morning. We are cast upon the shores of our bed linens from out of the infinite ocean of the night, left like debris as the dream recedes from us. We then must take up the burden of the mystery: one's condition as an embodied being in a world that is other than that being, that is in so many ways inert, sluggish, unresponsive to our thoughts and desires.

It is not surprising, then, that we can often detect an undertone of melancholy in the moment of waking—and precisely melancholy rather than some other shade of regret. For this feeling's configuration conforms to the two main points Freud uses to define melancholy. First, the loss that generates the melancholy of waking is not a loss that one can "get past" in any act of mourning, for it is reopened every day at the moment that we open our eyes. Second, the problem for Freud's patients, as he puts it, is that "a loss . . . has occurred, but one cannot see clearly what it is that has been lost" ("Mourning" 254), and for that reason cannot come to terms with it. Here Freud is speaking of the loss of a love object, but his words acquire a very different resonance when applied to the moment of waking. For what we have lost is our investment not in another person but in a mode of consciousness that has been our own; we have lost an extended and complex experience, and are unable to remember exactly what that experience consisted of or felt like. The result is a dim elusive sorrow that can never be resolved because it scarcely knows what it is sorrowing *for*.

The melancholy of waking is clearly, then, involved with our almost instantaneous forgetting of the mode that our consciousness inhabited during the night. Again, "almost" is a word that makes a difference, since if we wholly forgot our dream existence we would not even know of any loss. As it is, the loss comes just as much from a certain *kind of remembering* as it comes from the sense of having forgotten. This at least is Walter Benjamin's argument in his essay "On the Image of Proust." He writes:

> The day unravels what the night has woven. When we awake each morning, we hold in our hands, usually weakly and loosely, but a few fringes of the carpet of lived existence, as woven into us by forgetting. However, with our purposeful activity and, even more, our purposive remembering, each day unravels the web, the ornaments of forgetting. (576)

If sleep is a forgetting, waking is remembering. It is as if every time we awake we are in search of lost time, the time before we went to sleep. Yet this search does not have for Benjamin the kind of force we might expect: remembering is not a recovery of what is fully ourselves but a falling away from what we have learned through the night's forgetfulness. The reason for this unexpected twist is that Benjamin here is speaking of *purposive* remembering, which for him is a destructive activity: it restores to its usual banality what revealed itself to us in sleep as what he calls "the true surrealist face of existence." In this way remembering provides a specious comfort that covers over what we see when we forget how we are supposed to see. It overwrites the dim memory of our dream existence, which is soon obliterated entirely.

It is obliterated most effectively, perhaps, by the very tactic that we most commonly use to preserve it: we *tell* our dreams. Our aim in doing so is not really to communicate—we are vaguely aware that our auditors are polite but bored, as we will be bored when they tell us their dreams in turn. It is rather to preserve in words the memories of dreams that are already half dissolved, before they fade altogether into forgetfulness. But more than this, it is a project of control: we tell our dreams, Blanchot suggests, in order "to appropriate them and to establish ourselves, through our common speech, not only as the master of our dreams but as their principal actor, thereby decisively taking possession of this similar though eccentric being who was us over the course of the night" ("Dreaming, Writing" xxiv). Thus when a dream refuses to be contained within the protective circle of sleep, when it lingers in our memories and leaks into our waking lives, we wish for nothing more than to *explain* it, and in this way to subsume it into the comfortingly banal texture of our daily routines. This is a project that must always, necessarily, fail, and as such is the source of a secondary melancholy.

For those of us who insist on telling our dreams, Benjamin delivers some rather curious advice in a one-paragraph piece titled "Breakfast Room":

> A popular tradition warns against recounting dreams the next morning on an empty stomach. In this state, though awake, one remains under the spell of the dream. For washing brings only the surface of the body and the visible motor functions into the light, while in the deeper strata, even during the morning ablutions, the grey penumbra of dream persists and indeed, in the solitude of the first waking hour, consolidates itself.

This first half of the piece, with its warning about the consequences of an empty stomach, presents a peculiarly metabolic view of our relationship with our dreams. To some degree this is a view shared by Nietzsche, for whom it applies to waking states as well:

> Waking life does not have this *freedom* of interpretation possessed by the life of dreams, it is less inventive and unbridled—but do I have to add that when we are awake our drives likewise do nothing but interpret nervous stimuli and, according to their requirements, posit their "causes"? that there is no *essential* difference between waking and dreaming? . . . That our moral judgments and evaluations too are only images and fantasies based on a physiological process unknown to us, a kind of acquired language for designating certain nervous stimuli? That all our so-called consciousness is a more or less fantastic commentary on an unknown, perhaps unknowable, but felt text? (*Daybreak* 119–20)

This is something different from, say, Scrooge's insistence that Marley's apparition is only a dream caused by a badly digested piece of toasted cheese.

The relationship between the body's physiology and our psychology returns us to another touchstone of melancholy, the system of the humors, where temperament is a product of the proportions of certain fluids within the body. This antiquated notion is perhaps less startling to us in the age of antidepressants, but we may extend it—as perhaps Nietzsche intends us to do—from emotional disorders requiring treatment to all of our emotions. An emotion, after all, manifests itself as a physical *feeling*. The particular physical feeling that is the melancholy of waking may persist even after "purposive remembering" has kicked in to orient us. We do not, after all, wake up wholly or all at once, throwing off the bedclothes and leaping into action. Rather, we drag ourselves to the breakfast table, demanding our morning coffee "to wake ourselves up"—ignoring the fact that we are technically awake already. For the dream is still with us, whether we remember it or not. Our sense of self is clouded, not quite centered; our bodily metabolism is peculiarly altered; and there is the dim awareness of a lingering emotional entity—Nietzsche's "felt text." If dreams are constructed from the "remains of the day," the day is correspondingly invaded by the remains of the night. At least, this is so until we erect a barricade in the form of breakfast, filling the stomach, and consequently altering the chemistry of the spirit.

So the breakfast table is not only the place where we fill our stomachs but also the place where we empty our psyches of what Benjamin calls "the spell of the dream." However, according to Benjamin in the second half of "Breakfast Room," our attempts at control become a positive danger when undertaken on an empty stomach:

> In this condition, the narration of dreams can bring calamity, because a person still half in league with the dream world betrays it in his words and must incur its revenge. To express this in more modern terms: he betrays himself. He has outgrown the protection of dreaming naïveté, and in laying hands on his dream visages without thinking, he surrenders himself. For only from the far bank, from broad daylight, may dream be addressed from the superior vantage of memory. This further side of dream is attainable only through a cleansing analogous to washing, yet totally different. By way of the stomach. The fasting man tells his dream as if he were talking in his sleep.

We have here a betrayal and the revenge taken for that betrayal. The betrayal is that of narrative itself, because of the fact that the narrative of a dream is something other than the dream. Even Freud recognized this difference, though he appears occasionally to have forgotten it; and children of Freud that we are, we often conclude the narrations of our dreams by asking, "Now what do you suppose that means?" Yet the dream is not a meaning but an experience. Though meaning may be extracted from our dream narratives, neither narrative nor the meaning that is substituted for it is adequate to the *feel* of the dream, that "felt text"—which is nevertheless "unknown, perhaps unknowable." The narrative of a dream always falls short, just as the narrative of one's waking life would fall short if one attempted to tell it to an inhabitant of the dream realm. This shortfall is what betrays the dream—a betrayal that can be accomplished with impunity only when it is definitively removed from the experience it purports to account for: "only from the far bank," Benjamin says, "from broad daylight, may dream be addressed from the superior vantage of memory." Benjamin's irony is evident: "the superior vantage of memory" can be so called only when it is safely removed from the night's eccentricity, which throws into question the "purposive remembering" of the daylight world. If we are not so removed, the dream takes its revenge on those who try to narrate what is unnarratable.

The case is rather different, however, for authors, whose very business it is to narrate the unnarratable. Their strategies are put in place not to control the dream but to evoke it in themselves and in their readers. Repeatedly authors—John Gardner, Jorge Luis Borges, and John Banville, to name only a few—compare the act of writing to a waking dream. Writing on the side of night, on the side of dream, they are in the state described by Benjamin; for authors tell their tales from the perspective of the fasting man: in Kafkan terms, every artist is a hunger artist.

This contention is at the heart of a short story by that erratic artist Stephen King. "Harvey's Dream" is about the telling of a dream, and it takes place in a breakfast room. We experience it from the point of view of Harvey's wife Janet, who, as usual, is up on Saturday morning long before her husband—is in fact already making the deviled eggs for lunch. Then, in the story's opening sentence, "Janet turns from the sink and, boom, all at once her husband of nearly thirty years is sitting at the kitchen table in a white T-shirt and a pair of Big Dog boxers, watching her." Janet then has one of those moments when a woman looks at her unprepossessing husband and wonders if that's all there is. It's not just his aging scruffiness that bothers her but the fact that he is "sitting there silent and dopily contemplative instead of ready and raring, psyching himself up for the day" (86). This has been happening more and more often on weekends, and "she's afraid that when he retires it will be this way every morning, at least until she gives him a glass of orange juice and asks him . . . if he wants cereal or just toast" (85). The implication is that his fasting state contributes to his dopey contemplation—that is, that he is still in the grip of dream rather than fully arrived at "purposeful activity." And there is indeed a dream, from which Harvey had awakened screaming in the middle of the night. Janet, sleeping in another room because of her summer allergies, had heard nothing. When she asks him to tell her his dream, Harvey is not sure he wants to do this, to go back into the dream that terrified him. Janet encourages him with "They say if you tell your dreams they won't come true" (88)—a strategy that here will backfire horribly. The story becomes an example of how, in Benjamin's words, "the narration of dreams can bring calamity."

However, in this case the calamity does not come about for exactly the reasons that Benjamin suggests. While Harvey is indeed a "fasting man," he does not tell his dream "as if he were talking in his sleep." He is quite coherent as he describes an entirely realistic sequence: coming downstairs in the early morning, finding the deviled eggs in the refrigerator, seeing from the window an oddly stained dent in his hard-drinking neighbor's car, the phone ringing, and then the strangled, incoherent voice of one of their grown-up daughters finally getting out the word *killed,* and the realization that one of their other two daughters has died, been hit by the neighbor's car—at which point he woke to hear his own choked and incoherent voice asking *which one?* The bedside clock read 2:47 in the morning, and Harvey's waking state at this moment was a continuation of the incoherence that characterized his daughter's voice in the dream. It is only, perhaps, the buffer of the night's remainder that makes it possible for him now to tell his dream "from the far bank."

The significant twist in King's story is that it is not Harvey but Janet who is affected by the malaise of the dream. Immediately after she has urged Harvey to tell his dream, she reverses her earlier position: she is interested in what he has to say; he looks to her, physically, "as though he matters"; and she wonders, "Why, when I was just thinking that life is thin, should it seem thick?" (88). Her heart begins to beat faster, and she becomes acutely conscious of the shadows in the sunlit room: Harvey's shadow on the wall, that of the pepper mill on the table, and even those stretching out from the toast crumbs. Suddenly she does not want to hear the dream, wants life to be thin again, but Harvey is already talking. Horrified, Janet sees the dream's details—the deviled eggs, the dent in the neighbor's car—corroborated by reality. So when, in accordance with the dream sequence, the phone rings, "she would scream if she could draw breath" (94). But she is frozen—so it is Harvey who gets up and, in the last word of the story, says, "Hello?" At this point it hardly matters whether the phone call is, as Janet hopes it is, a wrong number, or whether the dream will replay itself all the way to its terrible conclusion. The point of the story is not factual but atmospheric; it is about the way that dreams can reach out into reality and transform it, thicken it ominously. But it is also about how words can do this.

For in the silence that follows Harvey's recital of his dream and before the telephone rings, Harvey says, "It's amazing, isn't it, how deep imagination goes? . . . A dream like that is how a poet—one of the really great ones—must see his poem. Every detail so clear and so bright" (94). In saying this he echoes something Janet has thought as she tries to put up mental reservations against one of the dream's details: "Dreams don't have to be logical, do they? Dreams are poems from the subconscious" (92). If this is so then, as Archibald MacLeish has famously said of poems, dreams "should not mean / but be." Far from reducing a dream to its meaning, we must experience it as a brief opening into Nietzsche's "unknown, perhaps unknowable, but felt text." And the word *text* here indicates that this may be the ultimate aim of a work of fiction as well. Lest life should dwindle into thinness, narrative makes it thick; and this need not at all be a comfortable thickness, but one that invites us to see shadows that we would rather ignore. Narrative's purpose is not to lay our dreams to rest but to evoke them, to prolong them, to make us feel their power in the very fibers of our bodies. When narrative works, when a text is *felt*, it produces that complex metabolic reaction in us that we call a work's "effect." As does King's story, putting us, whether we like it or not, in the position of Janet listening to Harvey's dream, which is also King's dream. And when the story ends, it is not really over—nor is this just because we are left to imagine what will be on the other end of the phone line. For when we put down the story we are in the position of someone who has dreamed and whose waking is disconcertingly incomplete; a fictive reality has seeped into our real body and altered its psychological metabolism. This is the common aftermath of reading. It can be summed up in these words from

Hermann Broch's novel *The Sleepwalkers,* which can be taken doubly, as pertinent to reading as they are to dreaming:

> Great is the fear of him who awakens. He returns with less certainty to his waking life, and he fears the puissance of his dream, which though it may not have borne fruit in action has yet grown into a new knowledge. An exile from dream, he wanders in dream. (303)

The territory of this wandering is no longer dream itself but rather what Benjamin, in "Breakfast Room," calls the "grey penumbra of dream." In the essay on Proust he uses a related metaphor: "a few fringes of the carpet of lived existence." What is being spoken of in such words as *penumbra* and *fringes* is a liminal state, dangerous to the degree that it allows the dream world to bleed into the waking one and thus to throw its "purposeful activity" into question.

LACAN'S WAKE-UP CALL

A good deal more than purposeful activity is thrown into question by Jacques Lacan in his eleventh seminar, where he analyzes the implications of a moment of waking:

> The other day, I was awoken from a short nap by knocking at my door just before I actually awoke. With this impatient knocking I had already formed a dream, a dream that manifested to me something other than this knocking. And when I awake, it is in so far as I reconstitute my entire representation around this knocking—this perception—that I am aware of it. I know that I am there, at what time I went to sleep, and why I went to sleep. When the knocking occurs, not in my perception, but in my consciousness, it is because my consciousness reconstitutes itself around this representation— that I know that I am waking up, that I am *knocked up.* (56)

Unlike Proust, Lacan here reconstitutes himself without undue difficulty; he does this by means of and around the perceptual stimulus of knocking. Yet he is subtle enough to detect in this incident a *double* reconstitution, one on either side of the divide between dreaming and waking. On one side, a dream representation forms around the knocking: "With this impatient knocking I had already formed a dream, a dream that manifested to me something other than this knocking." On the other side, another representation forms in which the knocking is not "something other" than itself but is recognized as knocking. Yet is not this recognition (re-cognition) itself a reconstituting? It is not just a matter, after all, of the perceptual experience of knocking but of assigning to that sensory perception its place in a familiar patterning. What one senses is not sound alone, it is *knocking*, it is someone at the door, it is time to wake up—all these associations to the perception are assigned to it by one's consciousness. In doing this, consciousness reconstitutes not the sound, which after all was already present; it reconstitutes what the sound *represents* to consciousness. Sound becomes consciousness-of-sound. That is to say, consciousness at this moment reconstitutes *itself*: "When the knocking occurs, not in my perception, but in my consciousness, it is because my consciousness reconstitutes itself around this representation"—or, as Lacan has already said, in a more extreme version, "I reconstitute my entire representation around this knocking." One's consciousness, then, is not only reconstituted "around" this representation, but also in a very real sense it *is* that representation. "[I am] able to sustain myself," Lacan goes on to say, "apparently only in a relation with my representation, which, apparently, makes of me only consciousness. A sort of involuted reflection—in my consciousness, it is only my representation that I recover possession of" (57). So there is a "symmetry," as Lacan calls it, between what occurs on both sides of "the gap itself that constitutes awakening" (57). On each side, a perceptual stimulus is subjected to a process of representation.[4]

This is a disconcerting enough conclusion, deftly undermining the privileged claims of one's own consciousness. For when one comes to consciousness at the moment of waking, one arrives there only through a process of representation. The representation of consciousness (the grammatical ambiguity is deliberate) differs, to be sure, from that attached by the dream to the perception of knocking; yet there is nothing in the two cases that would establish a clear difference between their *modes* of representation.

So far, we are dangerously close to the idea that *life is a dream*—

a formulation that Lacan explicitly warns against. For the symmetrical ambiguity of dreaming and waking life—summed up in this facile formulation—is only the first step in Lacan's project, which is an investigation of reality, in more than one version.

Lacan's dream is not described, but it plainly constitutes itself around the first version of the real here, which is the knocking. Perceptions are real, sound waves are real, before the dream represents them *otherwise*. In a parallel way, those perceptions are real before representation builds a certain consciousness around them—not otherwise but much as usual, attaching the suspended threads of memory and association to their habitual places. By so doing representation brings into being the habitual place, place of our inhabiting, that is our consciousness. We call this "waking up." Having finally awakened, we can do a reality check: "The real," Lacan says, "may be represented by the accident, the noise, the small amount of reality, which is evidence that we are not dreaming" (60). But notice that the noise here only *represents* the real—for Lacan has in mind a far more fundamental real, a Lacanian and capitalized Real.

Lacan explores the difference between these two versions of the real through an encounter that seems at first to emphasize their similarity: Freud's often-discussed "Dream of the Burning Child." Here it is in its entirety:

> A father had been watching beside his child's sick-bed for days and nights on end. After the child had died, he went into the next room to lie down, but left the door open so that he could see from his bedroom into the room in which his child's body was laid out, with tall candles standing round it. An old man had been engaged to keep watch over it, and sat beside the body murmuring prayers. After a few hours' sleep the father had a dream that *his child was standing beside his bed, caught him by the arm and whispered to him reproachfully: "Father, don't you see I'm burning?"* He woke up, noticed a bright glare of light from the next room, hurried into it and found that the old watchman had dropped off to sleep and that the wrappings and one of the arms of his beloved child's dead body had been burned by a lighted candle that had fallen on them. (*Interpretation of Dreams* 547–48)

Lacan first considers, with Freud, that the strange congruence of the dream with external reality may be accounted for by an awareness, and correct interpretation within the dream, of a perception outside the dream. For Lacan that perception is the knocking noise made as the candle overturns; for Freud it is the glare of the flames upon the dreamer's closed eyelids. But Lacan is not content with either explanation. He asks, *What is it that wakes the sleeper?*—and answers with a rhetorical question: "Is it not, *in* the dream, another reality?" (58). That reality is summed up in the dead child's sentence—a sentence that, Lacan says, "is itself a firebrand—of itself it brings fire where it falls" (69). This description reinforces the well-known link between the Lacanian Real and trauma, and indeed our usual expectations of trauma are amply fulfilled by this reproachful sentence and terrible vision. They produce in the father emotions so overwhelming that they break open the enclosure of sleep and wake him. It is a conflagration within that rouses the father to the material fire without. And yet Lacan goes on to say that "one cannot see what is burning, for the flames blind us to the fact that the fire bears . . . on the real" (59). The real here, in fact, goes beyond the specific trauma to a real that is expressed by the dynamic of the father's waking, of Lacan's waking, of waking in general.

Lacan concludes this section of his seminar as follows:

> How can we fail to see that awakening works in two directions—and that the awakening that re-situates us in a constituted and represented reality carries out two tasks? The real has to be sought beyond the dream—in what the dream has enveloped, hidden from us, behind the lack of representation of which there is only one representative. This is the real that governs our activities more than any other and it is psychoanalysis that designates it for us. (60)

The "lack of representation" cuts two ways. Representation is always involved with lack, with absence, re-presenting something that is not and perhaps cannot be present. But there is also a suggestion that, despite the prevalence of representation on either side of the divide that is waking, representation will always be lacking for "the real that governs our activities more than any other." While Lacan associates this real with Freud's notion of the drive, he admits that it must always "remain hidden from us." That which impels the very process of representation cannot itself be represented. We encounter its effects at fleeting intervals, of which "the gap . . . that constitutes awakening" (57) is one. Yet the encounter between dream and awakening is destined, Lacan says, to be "forever missed" (59). The real evades our representations of it even as it pervades our lives. We can never wake up to this reality, nor can we cease trying to do so. What Lacan says of the "missed reality" (58) depicted in the dream of the burning child may apply equally to the missed reality, forever missed, of our psychic lives: it is a reality "that can no longer produce itself except by repeating itself endlessly, in some never attained awakening" (58).

INTERMINABLE WAKING

Such an endlessly repeated awakening is the subject of Robert Irwin's 1983 novel *The Arabian Nightmare,* which has become something of a cult classic. In addition to being a novelist, Irwin is a historian of Arabic culture and has authored several books on that subject, including *The Arabian Nights: A Companion. The Arabian Nightmare* is both an homage to its illustrious predecessor and a dizzying extension of its implications. Superficially, Irwin's novel tells the story of a young Englishman, Balian, who arrives in Cairo both as a pilgrim to the shrine of Saint Catherine and as a spy. There he falls victim to a mysterious illness: every time he wakes, great quantities of blood come jetting out of his mouth and nostrils. It is feared that he might have the Arabian Nightmare, a disease whose victim suffers unimaginable agonies while asleep but remembers nothing of them upon waking. At any rate, it is clear that Balian needs treatment by a specialist in sleep diseases. The search for a cure—sometimes conducted within dreams and at other times while awake—is woven in with Balian's attempts, in his capacity as spy, to disentangle the many confusing intrigues that swarm about Cairo. These in turn are reflected in the narrative's own deliberate confusions, which continually and wittily disorient the reader—though in a particularly Oriental way.

At a couple of points Yoll, a professional storyteller who is both a character in the novel and claims to be narrating it, is identified as the author of *The Thousand Nights and One Night* (49, 277). The narrative that he purportedly creates indeed uses one of the most common strategies of *The Arabian Nights,* and that is *embedding.* For Scheherazade prolongs her life not so much by prolonging her stories as by opening them up, story within story; so that to listen to Scheherazade is to be continually moving inward, leaving the outer stories suspended, including the story of Scheherazade's own fate. The most extended series of embedded stories comes near the end of Irwin's novel, just when we are expecting things to reach their climax, bringing the revelation that will explain everything that has confused us before. This does not happen, of course. Instead the embedded stories here are bewilderingly similar to one another; each involves a monkey's riddle and a child raised by animals after being abandoned. The points that connect the stories and the variations that make them different (for instance, in the species of animal that adopts the foundling) become well nigh impossible to keep track of. The chapter titles in this section convey something of its effect on the reader—and perhaps something of the effect of Scheherazade's nighttime narratives on their auditor:

An Interlude—The Tale of the Talking Ape
The Interlude Concluded
The Interlude Concluded Continued
The Conclusion of the Continuation of the Interlude's Conclusion

Embedding is spoken of in various ways throughout the novel; most frequent, perhaps, is the metaphor of Chinese boxes, nested one within the other. When it becomes necessary for security reasons to kill Giancristoforo, an imprisoned Italian pilgrim, he is sent an actual Chinese box, one with frightening properties. When Giancristoforo opens it, it seems to be empty, but he hears "a scuffling sound, so soft it might have been a dream whispering in his head" (122). Lifting the box to his ear, he sees from the corner of his eye a long black-and-yellow worm raise itself over the side of the box and disappear. Immediately he feels a piercing pain in his head, along with a vision of proliferating recursivity: "The inside of Giancristoforo's skull was his cell, the inside of his cell his skull. And there was another box and, when opened, another worm and, inside that box, another cell that was also a skull and another worm, and another" until his brain is devoured by a "maggoty feast" (122–23).

Elsewhere Balian learns from his sleep teacher that dreams may also be embedded, so that "each dream carries within its womb another dream" (110). This is probably related to the "Zones" through which, according to this teacher, the sleeping mind descends:

> The most superficial was called the Zone of the Dog, a perplexing state barely distinguishable from wakefulness; the Zone of the Elephant was altogether more full-blooded and fantastic; then there was the Zone of the Lizard, which was less colourful and more conceptual; and so on and on. In each zone the space seemed smaller and the colours fewer. Somewhere in the heart of it all, his teacher told him, was a centre, infinitely small and dark, which could be approached only with great dread, the Zone of the Pebble. (109)

This center has an equivalent in the Chinese box of Giancristoforo's brain, as it is explored by those who are engineering its destruction—for the operants of this malign magic must themselves enter the victim's brain like worms. There they become aware of

> something small at the centre of the brain beyond reach of thought or memory, quite beyond conscious seizing—the primal matter of consciousness perhaps. One glimpsed from a great distance an area, brilliantly lit by flashes of lightning, in which tiny little men flickered and ran carrying letters, emblems and numbers amid blocks of flashing rods and colours. It was beyond meaning. (123)

These two versions of the center seem to be as different as possible from one another. The pebble is mute, hard, self-contained, unresponsive, in contrast to the busy, flickering, disseminatory realm of signs and stimuli. What unites them is their being "beyond meaning"—or perhaps that should be Being beyond meaning. Such depictions of a center evoke a whole battery of similar depictions, from *Heart of Darkness* to Derrida's "Structure, Sign, and Play." What all these resist, among other things, is the time-honored search for an orienting center, a search that proceeds from the outermost zones *inward.*

Irwin turns this version of embeddedness inside out, for Balian seeks not to probe deeper and deeper inside, in search of an ultimate secret; rather, he wants to move further and further *outside,* to leave behind the nightmarish paradoxes that threaten to engulf him. Balian wants, in short, to *wake up.* And he gets what he wants, to excess. The structure of embeddedness—one thing inside another—becomes, in a shift of perspective, one thing outside another. So, repeatedly, Balian wakes with relief from a dream, only to sense that something is not quite right about his surroundings; he then realizes that he has woken from one dream into another—and wakes again. At one point Balian passes through five consecutive awakenings (75–79), and there is no reason this series should stop there, or ever.

The city of Cairo is a perverse mapping of the dynamic that holds Balian in thrall. Just as he wants to wake up, so he wants to get outside of the city. But when he sets himself to do this, in a chapter hopefully titled "How to Leave Cairo," he finds himself unable to. A rhythm of sleeping and waking takes him over to the point that he can scarcely tell the difference: "He found himself no longer competent to distinguish always between the Cairo of nocturnal fantasy and the real city" (113). His steps grow slower; the twisted streets bring him back to his starting point, which he cannot always recognize as such (80). In an echo of Freud's use of Rome, we are told, "The city was like a disordered mind, an expression of archaic wishes and half submerged memories of vanished dynasties" (82–83). This at least promises a productive archaeology, excavating from the surface inward. Cairo, however, exemplifies an altogether more paradoxical space:

> Once—a momentary triumph, this—he walked or dreamt he walked out through the suburbs of Cairo and into the leafy paths and orchards on the northern edge of the city only to find, as he walked on, that the houses were appearing more frequently again and then more closely packed until indeed he was not far short of a Zuweyla Gate, centre of a second Cairo, the mirror of the first. (128–29)

We have already had the experience of a doubled Cairo as the book begins and then begins again in more or less the same words. Chapter 1, "The Way into Cairo," opens like this:

> "Cairo." The dragoman pointed ahead with obvious pride, though the city had been visible for over an hour now. (12)

Chapter 2, "Another Way into Cairo," opens (or reopens) like this:

> "Cairo." The guide pointed ahead, a skinny bronzed hand shooting out of his robes. (29)

The second version becomes progressively stranger until Balian awakens from it. This doubling, gothic though it may seem, has a certain comforting logic to Balian as, on the threshold of sleep, "he drowsily considered the warped symmetry of his experiences, dreams and facts all interlocked: two sultans, two beautiful women, two states of consciousness and so forth. Did everything in the universe have its corresponding partner in a pair, a left hand and right hand?" (59). This promise of symmetry becomes increasingly warped as the novel progresses, to the degree that it can hardly be called symmetry at all. For instance, at one point we get a description of the man with the Arabian Nightmare (who may or may not be Balian); he dreams of himself as a figure asleep on a bed, convulsing with pain:

> If he could only awaken the figure on the bed. If the figure on the bed could only awaken him.
> Then it seemed that the two of them were shaking each other awake, shivering with pain in the dawn light. . . . My brother, my double, he brings the Arabian Nightmare with him, they thought of each other. The figure tossing on the bed turns his attention away from them, though only with an effort, for logical space is getting smaller. (91)

Smaller indeed, in inverse proportion to the multiplying paradoxes of that internal space—a space that is quite different from a mirror's doubling or even from the more complex space of Chinese boxes. Chinese boxes, after all, are a comprehensible structure with at least the promise of a center. This promise, and this structure, is explicitly criticized by Balian's sleep teacher:

"They visualize life and dream as containers, and they think either that the dream is locked within the casket of waking life or that waking life is locked inside the dream. But, as we know, dream and life are not boxes and their relationships to one another must be seen in quite a different way." (137)

What is that different way? The sleep teacher does not explain. And though an explanation is implicit in the novel, we will have to approach it circuitously; and so I leave the question suspended, rather like one of Scheherazade's stories, until our education in dream has progressed a bit further.

Balian's own education literally takes place *in dream*, while he is asleep. In one such dream his teacher says, "You are no longer in the world of reality, a world which is governed by the laws of God and logic. No, you are in the Alam al-Mithal, which, being interpreted, is the World of Images or Similitudes" (60). The Alam al-Mithal is one of the planes of existence in the cosmology of Ibn Arabi (1165–1240) and other medieval Arab philosophers; it is the realm of the imagination, intermediate between body and spirit; and it is indeed, in some versions, the realm that one visits in dreams. Its "Images or Similitudes" may be juxtaposed with Blanchot's "region where pure resemblance reigns" in all the elusiveness of images. For Blanchot as well as Ibn Arabi this realm is not one that is safely sealed off by sleep. "Dreams are like the sea," Balian is told; "they sweep in to cover the brain in little waves and then withdraw, but the waves ripple out from something that is always there, the World of Images, the Alam al-Mithal" (108). When the brain is covered by this sea of images we dream, but this not to say that when we are not dreaming we are neatly separated from the Alam al-Mithal, for it is "always there." This is as much as to say that we are never wholly awake. Indeed, we may ask ourselves what it would *mean* to be "wholly awake." It is a question that is not entertained all that often, not even by sleep researchers, who should at least consider the presumed opposite of the state they are investigating.

One sleep researcher who does ask the question is Ian Oswald. A psychologist who relies strongly on electrophysiology, Oswald does not take the easy way out, of pointing to the disparities in brain wave patterns as recorded by a needle on a chart. He wants to speculate about states felt by the subject that might correspond to those patterns, and he does so, very cautiously, as follows:

> It appears that the sort of diffuse facilitation of cortical function which occurs in wakefulness as a result of ascending non-specific impulses from the reticular formation, might possibly be of a rather similar nature to that facilitation of selected topics, problems or perceived events which we call attention. The difference would lie in the latter being more selective or localized in its functional distribution. (71)

Attention, then, is postulated as the defining quality of wakefulness, though Oswald admits that attention may have various degrees of intensity within the waking state. He cautions that "we should use the word only to describe a function which has a selective and directed quality. We 'pay attention' to *something* (be it concrete or abstract)" (66). "Selective and directed" is of course the contrary to the dream experience, with rare and carefully cultivated exceptions; for the most part, as Lacan has indicated, we follow whatever the dream shows. Yet a selective and directed attention in the waking world is perhaps almost as rare, Oswald reminds us: "When we are awake we may become bored, our 'attention wanders,' we begin to day-dream, we may become drowsy and lose contact with reality. We may then experience dream fragments or dream sequences in light sleep, going through vivid experiences, including visual and auditory experiences, in a world of fantasy" (66). I would take Oswald's point even further: momentary lapses into fantasy, I would argue, are how thinking gets done. Just before he switches from the navel metaphor to the mycelium Freud says, "The dream-thoughts to which we are led by interpretation cannot, from the nature of things, have any definite endings; they are bound to branch out in every direction into the intricate network of our world of thought" (*Interpretation of Dreams* 525). He does not specify whether that "world of thought" is conscious or unconscious; and indeed perhaps a hard-and-fast distinction cannot be made. It is surely unnecessary to argue at length that creative thought, even in the sciences, is often carried out by way of dimly visualized shapes and relationships, or even by articulated images. Nor to recall how attention to abstract thought draws one inward, as it were, taking attention away from the concrete world. Nor how human beings, rarely living "in the moment," weave anticipations and memories into the present, so that fantasy receives at least as much attention as reality. And these lapses in attention are necessary, for to be wholly awake, to be wholly free of the Alam al-Mithal, would mean to be wholly without thought. We live our lives on the shoreline; and the sea within us obscures and reveals by turns a physical world to which we pay only intermittent attention. And this may be one of the ways in which Balian's sleep teacher wants him to think beyond the boxes.

It is a particular version of the boundary area between waking and dreaming that is the source of Yoll's stories, and consequently of the story we are reading. He finds his stories in the realm of hypnagogia. First he wanders at length through the city, "taking nothing in consciously, taking everything in somehow, floating in the airs of Cairo." Then

> he would return to his home on the edge of the Armenian Quarter and let himself drift, with his eyes shut, until images began to dance on his eyelids and a story began to form around them. Yoll's stories came, he claimed, from a twilight area, somewhere between conscious creation and the seethings of pure nonsense. (51)

We return, then, to a concern about the shape of stories.

A common notion of the narrative impulse, the impulse to tell stories about ourselves and read the stories of others, is that through shaping events we give them meaning. *The Arabian Nights* and *The Arabian Nightmare* both challenge this comforting notion, as this shaping itself becomes associated with death. The point of Scheherazade's tale-telling, we know, is to stave off death through narrative. This she does through embeddedness and—another common strategy of prolongation—the tendency of one story to evoke another that resembles it. Thus she ensures that the flow of stories will never end, will last as long as is necessary to prolong her life. King Shahryar's interest must be maintained. Yet that very interest is impelled toward death—not Scheherazade's death, for which it substitutes, but the death that is needed to reveal the shape of a character's life. As Walter Benjamin puts it in his essay "The Storyteller":

> [For any character in a novel] the "meaning" of his life is revealed only in his death. But the reader of a novel actually does look for human beings from whom he derives the "meaning of life." Therefore he must, no matter what, know in advance that he will share their experience of death: if need be their figurative death—the end of the novel—but preferably their actual one. How do the characters make him understand that death is already waiting for them—a very definite death at a very definite place? That is the question which feeds the reader's consuming interest in the events of the novel. (100–101)

Only when the story ends, along with all the stories it contains and resembles, will its shape be fully manifest, and not until then. So the prostitute Zuleyka tells Balian, "Similarly, every story has its death wish, rushing on to become silence" (260). "Similarly" because this is a parallel case of another rush to the finish, that of his penis, which she is training him to resist. The story's death wish too is to be resisted—as indeed the Freudian death wish resists itself:

> It is as though the life of the organism moved forward with a vacillating rhythm. One group of instincts rushes forward so as to reach the final aim of life as quickly as possible; but when a particular stage in the advance has been reached, the other group jerks back to a certain point to make a fresh start and so prolong the journey. (*Beyond the Pleasure Principle* 40–41)

This prolongation is like Scheherazade's, and the "journey" is like the endless reiterations of Balian's attempts to leave Cairo:

> It is so easy to get lost and so often in wandering round a strange city, without intending it, a man will return to where he started and yet in returning to that place he will fail to recognize it as his starting point, so that when he picks up his steps again, he starts from the same place for the first time. (80)

No wonder, then, that "every visitor finds it difficult to leave Cairo. It unfolds itself like a story that will never end" (130). Such a story is

The Arabian Nightmare. One cannot assert that it will never end because it is infinitely extended or extensible—for of course one comes to a last page and closes the book's cover. Rather, as we have seen in the description of Yoll's hypnagogic creation, the story emerges out of an infinity, the sea of Alam al-Mithal; and it returns to that infinity as the story is being read.

For *The Arabian Nightmare*'s paradoxes extend to the very act of reading it, or indeed reading any work of fiction. The novel's first words are these: "For a long time I used to go to bed early." These echo, of course, the famous first words of Proust's *Remembrance of Things Past.* In that work, they are immediately followed by the passage we have already looked at in the context of falling asleep while reading. You will recall that Irwin's narrator follows up his first sentence along the same lines:

> Though the art of reading is not widespread in these parts, I confess myself to be a devotee of the practice and, in particular, of reading in bed. It is peculiarly pleasant, I have found, to lie with the book propped up against the knees and, feeling the lids grow heavy, to drift off to sleep, to drift off in such a way that in the morning it seems unclear where the burden of the book ended and my own dreams began. (11)

These proclivities of the narrator have prompted him to write "a narrative designed to be read in bed," and *The Arabian Nightmare* is that narrative. As it approaches the last few pages, the author admits that there is less and less room to resolve the problems that have proliferated as the novel has unfolded and refolded into itself: "All I can hope is that, to return to the theme with which I opened, finally it will be unclear where the burden of my book ended and the contents of your dreams began" (261). This is a hope that is bound to be fulfilled, since it is *always* unclear where the book ends and the reader's part begins. Any book takes place not merely at the level of the letters on the page but also in the spaces between. An explicit case of these "spaces between" precedes the scene, already discussed, of the Chinese box that, opened, eats Giancristoforo's brain. The coloration of the black-and-yellow worm that emerges from the box is not an arbitrary one: it is the coloration of the ambiguous note that accompanies the box, which to Giancristoforo's fevered imagination reveals something of what all writing entails:

> The ink seemed very black and the paper brilliant yellow. As he stared he saw that between the black lay great chasms of yellow that yawned beneath the writing, sandstone gorges in which one stood, lost in their immensity and marveling at the black letters that raced and danced above. (121)

This is of course Arabic writing, and so the "whorls of script" produce a "worm-like after-image" (121–22). But writing may produce other images too, associations, resemblances, thoughts that accompany the words of the text but do not simply mirror them. And this too is the Alam al-Mithal, albeit a particular and personal one.

In a book that his sleep teacher says contains "the source of all stories" (163), Balian reads this:

> Some people say that every skull contains within itself its own sea of dreams and that there are millions upon millions of these tiny oceans. They adduce as proof the fact that if you put your ear against the ear of a friend and listen closely, you may hear the sea beating against the wall of the skull. But how can the finite contain the infinite? (24)

Leaving aside the "proof," we begin to understand that the paradox in question here is resolved not by logic but by anyone's daily practice: within the finite circumference of the skull is the "intricate network of our world of thought," which cannot, Freud says, "have any definite endings." Similarly, within any finite book are cracks and chasms—some deliberate, some not—into which flow images and resemblances from its reader's sea of dreams.

Thus the narrator delivers on his promise to create a narrative designed to be read in bed, and perhaps cannot help but do so. But who is this narrator? I have said that Yoll is the purported narrator of the story—which is to say that he is not really the narrator, an implication that becomes a certainty when he is killed about three-quarters of the way through. The "real" narrator is revealed only at the book's ending. There has been a resolution, followed by a false complication, followed by another resolution, and now all the characters are happily banqueting together. Then someone upsets a glass. Balian watches it drift to the floor without shattering and recognizes a sign that he is dreaming. At that moment he wakes up, for the last time in the book:

> Someone was shaking him awake.
> The hand that was shaking him felt curiously insubstantial.
> "Wake up," said the Ape. "I want to tell you another story. . . ."
> (280)

Here is our narrator, then, an unexpected one. And—leaving aside the disturbing implications of that "insubstantial"—the question now is, who is the Ape?

We have encountered an ape—if not, perhaps, the Ape—earlier in the story, sitting on Yoll's shoulder. This ape is perfectly substantial, spitting morsels of undigested food into the hair and shoulders of its owner, and thus earning him the sobriquet Dirty Yoll. Again, when Balian opens the book that is said to contain the source of all stories, the first thing he reads is the warning "Beware of the Ape!" with no further explanation. We may approach an explanation, however, by observing the ways in which the ape is used as a figure of speech in the novel: Balian tests dream figures to see "how well they can ape reality" and is told that "nature apes art" (203). This is a venerable and familiar trope, in which the ape emblematizes the principle of mimicry, imitation, false resemblance—or, in Ibn Arabi's terms, the principle of similitude. This is a principle that holds sway not only in the world of dreams but in waking life as well; for it is through similitudes that we make sense of the world. An "explanation" is effective because it translates something unknown into something known and familiar[5]—and similar: (A + x). So Zuleyka, summing up, can say, "To speak figuratively, the Ape rules the world" (259).

The Ape, then, has us entangled in an endless web of similitudes, extending infinitely far into our world of thought, which after all is the only world we know. It is all very well to say "Beware of the Ape!" but that is not to say that we can escape it, any more than Balian can escape from Cairo. Like Cairo, our minds are a blend of reality and fantasy, shifting between them in ways that cannot always be distinguished. We can never be sure, in fact, that we are wholly awake.

There is always a waking beyond our waking, and another waking beyond that, so that the struggle to awaken becomes an interminable one. Somehow we find ourselves within a sequence of similitudes, one inside the other, without quite knowing or recalling how we came to be there. We try to get outside the sequence, to move beyond the approximations of similitude to a clear and perfect waking. But each time we seem to wake it is only to find that we have not yet done so, that we are still in the realm of similitude, and that our waking, such as it is, is destined to be interminable.

What the Arabian philosophers call similitude can be related to what Lacan, in his eleventh seminar, has called representation. Impelled by drives that must remain hidden from us, a process rather than an object to be denominated, this is the real that governs all of our approximated realities. Its result is an interminable process from which we can never wake completely. So Lacan in conversation can state: "Even in absolute awakening, there is still an element of dream which is precisely the dream of awakening. We never wake up: desires keep dreams alive. . . . Life is something completely impossible which can dream of absolute awakening" ("Improvisation"; translation mine).

FOUR

Sleepwaking

If, as Lacan indicates, we never wake up absolutely even when we think we are absolutely awake, it follows that an element of dream accompanies us always, whether or not we are not conscious of it. So Blanchot can say, in *The Writing of the Disaster*, "There is no stop, there is no interval between dreaming and waking. In this sense it is possible to say: never, dreamer, can you awake (nor, for that matter, are you able to be addressed thus, summoned)" (35). The possible dissolution of the interval or boundary line between dreaming and waking has repeatedly troubled philosophers, perhaps most famously in the conundrum expressed by Zhuangzi in the fourth century B.C.E.:

> Once upon a time, I, Zhuangzi, dreamed I was a butterfly, fluttering hither and thither, to all intents and purposes a butterfly. I was conscious only of following my fancies as a butterfly, and was unconscious of my individuality as a man. Suddenly, I awoke, and there I lay, myself again. Now I do not know whether I was then Zhuangzi dreaming I was a butterfly, or whether a butterfly is now

dreaming it is me. Between Zhuangzi and a butterfly there is necessarily a barrier. This is called transformation of things.

The translation I have used (slightly modified) is by Xiaoqiang Han,[1]
and matters of translation are important here. Han has found it necessary to make his own translation rather than to accept philosophical implications that arise speciously from certain English phrasings.
Even his version, as he would be the first to admit, suggests a more
stable self than does the original, affixing a certain signature with
"I, Zhuangzi" that is carried forward in the passage's repetition of
"I." So it is "I" that was a butterfly—rather than "there was a butterfly," another possible phrasing—and perhaps this must be so when
the whole episode is reported from the hither, human side of the division between philosopher and butterfly. It is significant that this division is very much to the fore as the passage ends: most translations
stop at Zhuangzi's expression of doubt. If that doubt has to do with
whether he has been the dreamer or is now the dreamed there is no
doubt about the difference, the "barrier" between life as a butterfly
and life as a man. This butterfly is a bit like Thomas Nagel's bat:[2] it
poses a fundamental challenge to our ability to imagine a radically
alien other. Whatever remembrance of the butterfly-life is now held
by the human being can only be in human terms.

　　If Zhuangzi's purpose is, through the anecdote of a dream, to
make a Daoist point about the irrevocable differences between
"things,"[3] that is not the point that readers in the West have taken
from it: the vehicle for Zhuangzi's point has become a point in itself,
a point very much in contention. An awareness of the strange division between different forms of life has been replaced by an awareness of how difficult it is to establish the difference between waking
and dreaming states; for each of these states is convincing while we
are in it, as are for Zhuangzi the life of a butterfly and the life of a
man. West reads East in these terms, doubtless, because the difference between waking and dreaming states has repeatedly unsettled
Western thought—beginning perhaps with Socrates, who asks in
Plato's *Theaetetus,* "How can you determine whether at this moment
we are sleeping, and all our thoughts are a dream; or whether we are
awake, and talking to one another in the waking state?" (158b). This

venerable debate has recently been reopened by cognitive researchers such as Llinas and Paré, who have determined that the brain responds to the stimuli of dreams in the same way that it responds to the stimuli of waking perceptions.

I am not ambitious enough, or rash enough, to try to settle the ongoing debate about whether, or how, waking life can be distinguished from dreaming life. Rather, I want to consider the ways in which, as Blanchot implies, there is always an element of dream in our waking lives. I will do this through the work of a number of authors who, in various ways, have engaged with this interface. And indeed, as I have argued throughout this book, the work of an author itself takes place on such an interface. It is perhaps not surprising, then, that in the course of the debate over the relationship between waking life and dream life, that relationship is sometimes presented in terms of what happens to the reader of a book. For example, in a chapter titled "Chuang-Tzu's Doubt," Bert States takes on Daniel Dennett's essay "Are Dreams Experiences?" In this essay, Dennett assigns a privileged position to physical evidence that something is happening to the dreamer: "Whereas nightmares accompanied by moans, cries, cowering, and sweaty palms *would* be experiences, bad dreams in repose (though remembered in agony) would not be" (169). States counters this with the example of a man reading a book in a hotel lobby:

> You can see he's awake and intentionally doing something, if only turning pages. The part you can't see is his mind converting the words on the page into mental images of characters and events. Would you doubt that he was reading even though you detect no moans, cries, cowering, or sweaty palms to verify that he was? Probably not; because he is awake, though perfectly motionless, you safely assume that he is reading *something*, not only a book but a book *about* something and that these somethings are passing into his brain as thoughts, though you have no idea what they are. (*Seeing in the Dark* 78)

Dreams, States argues, work in a similar way. Such things as rapid eye movements and electrical impulses in the brain are evidence enough that a *mental* experience is being had. This cognitive evidence is comparable to reading's ocular saccades and measurable electrical activity in the brain (not to mention the occasional turned page), though for Dennett this might still not be sufficient for the act of reading to meet his criteria of an "experience," any more than dream does.

The book metaphor is used rather differently by Schopenhauer in *The World as Will and Presentation* as he considers, once again, the question of whether there is a clear distinction between dreams and waking life:

> Life and dreams are pages from one and the same book. Reading in context is what we call actual life. But when the current hour for reading (the day) has ended, and the time for recuperation has arrived, then we still often leaf idly through the book, turning this or that page without order or interconnection: often it is a page already read, often one still unfamiliar, but always from the same book. A single page read in this way is, of course, removed from the context of continuous reading. Yet it will not seem for that reason so very deficient with respect to the latter, when we consider that the whole of a continuous reading itself begins and ends with as much spontaneity, and is accordingly to be viewed as only a longer single page. (48)

"Interconnection" (and disconnection) is emphasized here because Schopenhauer is taking on Kant's assertion that "the interconnection of presentations in accordance with the law of causality distinguishes life from dreams" (46).[4] Schopenhauer points out that connections seem perfectly logical while a dream is taking place, and that the only disconnection involved is at the moment of waking—which, I might add, need not be privileged over the disconnection that happens when we fall asleep. Moreover, he argues, in waking life "we are in no way in a position to follow, link by link, the causal interconnection between all experienced events and the present moment" (46). Even at the time we are having an experience we can hardly be aware of all the connections that have been brought into play to make it happen. Indeed, it is the complex web of connections of all kinds— perceptual, emotional, mnemonic—that distinguishes an "experience" from the bare-bones "law of causality." And when recalled, any "experience" in waking life may present itself to memory in a form as fragmented and elusive as a dream experience, with the same temptation to transform it, after the fact, into a coherent narrative. In this sense, then, dreams *are* experiences, and correspondingly our experiences while awake may be accompanied by the dynamics that prevail in dreams.

DISQUIET

"I'm almost convinced that I'm never awake," writes Fernando Pessoa in *The Book of Disquiet*. "I don't know if I'm not dreaming when I live, if I don't live when I dream, or if my dreaming and living aren't mixed, intersected things, out of which my conscious being is formed by interpenetration" (146). Actually, to be precise, these words must be attributed to Bernardo Soares, whose name is given in the book as the work's author. Soares is one of a number of heteronyms employed by Pessoa in his writing—or perhaps it would be more accurate to say that they employ him. More than pseudonyms, the heteronyms have their own biographies, physical descriptions, and psychological profiles; these are reflected in the nature of the writing they produce. They are at times at odds with one another, producing articles critical of each other's work. Nor is this merely a witty game. It was upon waking on the morning of March 8, 1913, that Pessoa found himself visited—in what form remains unclear— by Alberto Caeiro, the first of the heteronyms; the effect on his writing was instantaneous:

> I went up to a high commode and, taking a piece of paper, began to write, standing, as I write whenever I can. And I wrote thirty or 50 poems all at once, in a kind of ecstasy the nature of which I will never be able to define. It was the triumphal day of my life. (xii)

Other heteronyms soon followed, each with his own distinct personality and writing style. In many ways the modernist forerunner of postmodern challenges to a stable identity, Pessoa—whose name in Portuguese means "person"—is rather like a Zhuangzi who dreams not of one butterfly but of a multitude. And indeed the heteronyms reproduce a certain dynamic of dream:

I've always been an ironic dreamer, unfaithful to my internal promises. I always enjoyed, as if I were another, a stranger, the defeats of
my divagations, accidental witness to what I thought I was. . . .

If it weren't for constant dreaming, living in a perpetual alienation, I would be happily able to call myself a realist, that is, an individual for whom the external world is an independent nation. But
I prefer not to call myself anything, to be who I am with a certain
obscurity and to have with myself the malice of not knowing how to
foresee myself. (159)

While the dreaming here may seem to be merely a figure for a certain
contemplative nature, it becomes apparent throughout *The Book of
Disquiet* that it is real dreams—and the dream of reality—that preoc-
cupy Soares, as has already been indicated by his words about the
interpenetration of the two realms. Soares, of all the heteronyms,
is the one who corresponds most closely to the facts of Pessoa's life;
accordingly, his meditations may be closest to Pessoa's thinking, at
least at the time of writing. An accountant in an office located in
the same area of Lisbon in which Pessoa worked as an accountant,
Soares writes about his humdrum reality and the ways in which it is
continually mingled with waking dreams, to the degree that reality
itself is called into question:

I've discovered that I always think about and pay attention to two
things at the same time. All of us must be that way to some extent.
Some impressions are so vague that only afterward, because we remember them, do we know we had them; of those impressions, I
think, are formed a part—the internal part, perhaps—of everyone's
double attention. It happens with me that the two realities I attend to
stand out equally. My originality consists in that. (76)

Soares follows this with a description of how at the same time he is
making his entries in the company's record book and observing the
deck of a ship voyaging to the Orient. This is something other than a
daydream of the sort described, for instance, in John Ashbery's "The
Instruction Manual"; for daydreaming typically obliterates the real
world and substitutes another. But Soares sees both worlds "with the
same attention. . . . The two things are equally clear, equally visible
before me" (76). If attention is the mark of a waking state, Soares's

double attention throws into question the division between waking and dreaming, in a way that recalls Zhuangzi's dilemma: "Even my dream," he says, "castigates me. Within it I achieved such lucidity that I see each thing I dream as real" (84).

One of the most eloquent renderings of this double attention is "In the Forest of Alienation," a piece published by Pessoa in his lifetime and signed with his own name. However, it was also included in the trunkful of manuscripts marked as destined for *The Book of Disquiet*; for not only does it explicitly reference disquiet, but it does so in such a way as to link it to the interpenetration of waking and dream worlds. "I know I woke up and that I'm still sleeping," the piece begins. And then:

> In a lucid, heavily incorporeal torpor, I stagnate, between dream and wakefulness, in a dream that is a shadow of dreaming. My attention floats between two worlds and blindly sees the depths of a heaven; and these depths interpenetrate, mix together, and I don't know where I am or what I'm dreaming.
>
> . . . I float in the air between being awake and being asleep, and another species of reality arises. I, in the middle of it, don't know which is which.

That species of reality is an Edenic forest filled with flowers. Yet this species of reality does not obliterate another one, which continues to be present to the double attention of someone called "I." The two realities coexist "like two plumes of smoke that blend together." At intervals, we are told, "I feel a slow wind blow away some smoke, and that smoke is the clear and dark vision of the bedroom in which I am now, with these vague pieces of furniture and curtains and with their nocturnal torpor" (177–78). "I" too is doubled, as he strolls with a nameless woman. She is to some degree a fantasy lover, a prelapsarian Eve for this Eden. But she is also something more complex: "Just as the landscape became two—of the reality it was, and of illusion—so were we obscurely two, neither of us knowing well if the other wasn't himself, if the vague other were living" (182). This strange ontology is a reflection of the dream state, where "behind my attention someone dreams with me. . . . Perhaps I am nothing but the dream of that Someone who doesn't exist" (178). If, as Lacan suggests, one's position in the dream is that of someone who follows, the question arises of *what* is being followed: Who, or what, is doing the dreaming that gives the dream subject its being? Less convincing than Zhuangzi's butterfly might lead us to believe, the dream being of this couple is characterized by Pessoa in these words: "Our life had no inside. We were outside and other" (179). Of course much the same thing might be asserted of the philosopher who ostensibly "has" the butterfly dream. Dream, then, interpenetrates the waking world with its subtle alienations.

And the reverse is also true: the real world penetrates the dream world, undermining its Edenic promise. However differently its dynamics might seem to work, however detached from a conscious selfhood, the dream is made up of the remains of the day, of the daylight world. There is no absolute escape from the burden of existing in that reality: "it pained us. . . . Because, despite what it had of calm exile, all that landscape reminded us of being of this world" (181). And so within the lush forest—made up of memories of other forests not originating in dream—the dreamers pass "hours of happy disquiet" (180). It is a disquiet made up of numerous emotions. There is a curious nostalgia for the present: "I, who far from that landscape almost forget it, am the one who on having it feel nostalgia for it, am the one who as he walks through it weeps for it and aspires toward it" (178). There is a fatigue that is "the shadow of a fatigue. It comes to us from far off, like our idea of having our lives" (181). There is even tedium, "the tedium of being," since in the midst of this "paradise of absence" there is the pressure of presence, of "having to be something, reality or illusion" (182). For illusion is only "another species of reality" (177) and makes no fewer demands on our existence than other such species. Waking, then, is not for Pessoa such a greatly changed state as it may sometimes seem. It is accompanied by the same disquiet that he senses in his dreams—which, again, are not so different from his waking moments as he might wish. Both states ask of him a continued existence, an oppressive *il y a* that is found in waking life and dreams alike.

Pessoa's influence has been widespread, more so than has generally been recognized until recently.[5] The most remarkable instance of that influence is doubtless the Italian writer Antonio Tabucchi, who as a young student in Paris picked up a used copy of Pessoa's poems at a bookstall. It changed his life. Adopting Portugal as his spiritual home, he became professor of Portuguese literature at the Universities of Pisa and Siena, specializing in Pessoa,[6] and worked in Lisbon for the Italian diplomatic service. At the same time he became one of Italy's leading contemporary writers. In Tabucchi's novels and short stories, characters repeatedly talk about Pessoa, and it is not uncommon for Pessoa to appear in person. But beyond these superficial references, Tabucchi's literary work shows a more profound kinship with Pessoa: their shared fascination with the permeable boundary between waking life and dream, and the implications of this for questions of the self and the other.

Of Pessoa's *Book of Disquiet* Tabucchi has this to say, in a "Post-face" to the French edition titled *La Poétique de l'insomnie*:

> Bernardo Soares does not dream because he does not sleep. He "un-sleeps," to use one of his own expressions; he frequents the space of hyperconsciousness and of free consciousness that precedes sleep. A sleep which, however, never arrives. *The Book of Disquiet* is an enormous insomnia. . . . His insomnia, leaving behind it the psychoanalyst's couch, is intertwined with the feverish vigil of '40s existentialism, with Levinas and with Blanchot. (268; translation mine)[7]

Blanchot provides the epigraph for Tabucchi's novel *Indian Nocturne*:

> Those who sleep badly seem to a greater or lesser degree guilty: what do they do? They make the night present. (*Space* 265)

As its title indicates, *Indian Nocturne* takes place almost entirely at night, leaving out the obviously necessary transitions to get from one place within India to another, from one night to another. For the night of this novel is a metaphysical one, and it is made present through a kind of insomnia. What Tabucchi has said of *The Book of Disquiet* holds true of his own book, too, according to his "Author's Note":

> As well as being an insomnia, this book is also a journey. The in-
> somnia belongs to the writer of the book, the journey to the person
> who did the travelling.

The person who did the traveling, at first nameless, is in India to find
his missing friend Xavier; the journey unfolds as each location provides a clue that takes him to the next one. These locations are listed
in order at the beginning of the book following the "Author's Note,"
which explains that the list is included to clarify the events of the narrative, and also in the unlikely event that a reader may someday want
to retrace this journey. But there are other effects as well, on both
sides of the waking/dreaming interface. The geographical specificity
of the locations is in accordance with Tabucchi's tendency to insert
into his most dreamlike novels a material element that keeps them
from becoming wholly dreams, only *like* dreams. In *Requiem,* for example, subtitled *A Hallucination,* the characters spend a good deal of
time eating traditional Portuguese dishes, discussing food, and even
obtaining recipes. So in *Indian Nocturne* each location is described
in realistic detail, with its distinctive atmosphere and incident. However, each place so described is, in the absence of transitions, curiously detached from the others; and this creates an effect that begins
to pull toward the dreamlike. Through spatial location we are given
something of the strangeness of temporal location: we move in time
through a reiterated "now" that is also a reiterated "here." Yet it can
also be argued that nothing is reiterated—that at any moment that
we move from one place to another, everything changes. And these
disjunctions, which we live with unquestioningly in our waking
hours, can be linked to the disjunctions of dream, where we find ourselves subjected to abrupt changes: "And then I was no longer on the
ship; it had turned into a kind of library." A journey intensifies our
awareness of disjunctions that are elided by the benevolent habit of
viewing our lives as if from the outside, as a linked sequence, a habit
that we call "home." When we travel, though, we may come to realize
that in a sense we are always traveling. So in the fourth location of
Tabucchi's novel, the Railway Retiring Rooms in Bombay, a man in
the bed next to the narrator's asks wearily, "What are we doing inside these bodies." The narrator replies, "Perhaps we're travelling in

them"—and then, "Perhaps they're like suitcases: we carry ourselves around" (26).

What exactly we are carrying—what makes up "ourselves"— is however very much in question here. The disquiet of insomnia in both Pessoa's book and Tabucchi's unravels any stable concept of self. Late at night in a railway station, the narrator consults a tiny deformed creature who claims the power of divination. But she cannot tell him of his future, of the success or failure of his quest; for, she says, "You are someone else" (53). He is elsewhere, apparently on a ship that she sees; without a self he has no future to be told. Rimbaud's *"Je" est un autre* is increasingly literalized as the book draws to its close. The narrator, Rossignol, finds that his friend now calls himself Mr. Nightingale. And the last location of the book is the scene of a final dislocation. Dining on the terrace of a luxury hotel in Goa, the narrator tells the woman he is dining with about a friend who, it seems, has been seeking him throughout India without success. As he concludes his account of his friend's futile search, he sees, at the other end of the terrace, a man dining with a woman. The man meets his gaze across the woman's shoulder; and it is as if the narrator, whoever he may be, is looking into a mirror. He reacts with little surprise, pays his bill, and leaves with his dining companion.

While there is much that can be said, and has been said, about the self-as-other, perhaps the most apt commentary for this novel is provided by Blanchot, whose initial epigraph can be matched with this . . . epitaph:

> [In dream] the show is being put on for someone who is not watching it in person and who does not have the status of a subject who is present. If dreams seem so foreign, it is because we find ourselves in the situation of strangers; and we are strangers precisely because the dreamer's self lacks any sense of true self. One could almost say that there is nobody in the dream and therefore, in a certain fashion, that there is nobody to dream it; hence the suspicion that when we are dreaming there is also someone else dreaming, someone who is dreaming us and who in turn is being dreamed by someone else, a premonition of that dream without a dreamer that would be the dream of the night itself. ("Dreaming, Writing" xxiv–xxv)

Tabucchi's *Nocturne* is also a dream of the night itself—in the words of Blanchot's epigraph, it makes the night present. At the same time what is made present is only a series of absences: the unattainable self, the jump-cut continuity, and even the dreamer who is the author, a "nobody" who disappears in an infinite regress. In an interview with Bernard Comment, Tabucchi stated:

> Writing is like opening a door, beyond which opens another door and the doors never come to an end. This is why my characters return, why they tug at my coat, want to go on being heard; why, in Freudian terms, I don't "stop grieving," why the universe which I've made for myself . . . is, from now on, my own universe, and I myself no longer know whether I am author or character, theatrical director or actor in it. What difference does it make after all? (Trentini 94)

Blurring the differences is characteristic as well of Tabucchi's *Requiem: A Hallucination*. Hallucination is a deception that appears to be a reality; it inevitably prompts us to ask by what signs we can distinguish the reality from its appearance. This is of course a variation on Zhuangzi's doubt. In *Phenomenology of Perception*, Maurice Merleau-Ponty reminds us that patients suffering from hallucinations can figure out *logically* that what they are really seeing cannot be real; at the same time, he puts forward an unsettling suggestion, that

> hallucination and perception are modalities of one single primordial function, through which we arrange round about us a setting of definite structure, through which we are enabled to place ourselves at one time fairly and squarely in the world, and at another marginally to it. The patient's existence is displaced from its centre, . . . expending its substance in isolation creating a fictitious setting for itself. *But this fiction can have the value of reality only because in the normal subject reality itself suffers through an analogous process.* (342)

Given the choice of being "at one time fairly and squarely in the world, and at another marginally to it," Pessoa has chosen to be "diagonal to the rectangular certitude of life" (180). It is perhaps for this reason, among others, that the narrator of *Requiem* has been given an improbable appointment to meet the long-dead Portuguese writer at twelve o'clock. Such a thing is possible only in hallucination, or in literature. Both of these, we discover, have combined to generate the narrator's ambiguous condition, a condition that he is himself at a loss to explain: "My problem is that I don't know why I'm here, it's as if it were all a hallucination," he says to the first person he encounters in this novel's pages, who seems curiously familiar to him. He places him then by tracing his steps back to an earlier location:

> Do you know Azeitão? Well, that's where I was, at a friend's house, in their garden, sitting under a big tree there, a mulberry tree I think, I was stretched out in a deckchair reading a book I particularly like and then I suddenly found myself here, ah, now I remember, it was in *Book of Disquiet*, you're the Lame Lottery-Ticket Seller who was always bothering Bernardo Soares, that's where I met you, in the book I was reading under the mulberry tree in the garden of a farmhouse in Azeitão. (14)

If writing, in Tabucchi's view, is something that blurs the differences between being "inside" and "outside" a work of fiction in a way that is akin to hallucination, the same is here being said of reading. "Today is a very strange day for me," the narrator muses; "I'm dreaming but what I dream seems to me to be real" (17). Perhaps this is always true of dreams while we are in them, but something more complex than dream is going on here. At one point the narrator is diagnosed by an old Gypsy woman who is reading his palm:

> Listen, my dear, she said, this can't go on, you can't live in two worlds at once, in the world of reality and the world of dreams, that kind of thing leads to hallucinations, you're like a sleepwalker walking through a landscape with your arms outstretched, and everything you touch becomes part of your dream, even me, a fat old woman weighing twelve and a half stone, I can feel myself dissolving into the air at the touch of your hand, as if I was becoming part of your dream too. (25)

And of course she *is* part of his dream, or his hallucinated fiction.

That fiction is made up of a series of conversations with two kinds of people. Some of them, we are told, are "certain people who exist only in my memory" (17)—which is to say they no longer exist and must be encountered one last time in order to be laid finally to rest.

Others, nameless but capitalized like the Old Gypsy Woman, have a generic force. They exemplify another aspect of the book—not a requiem but an homage to Portugal; indeed, Tabucchi wrote the novel in Portuguese, entrusting the translation into Italian to Sergio Vecchio. So the novel becomes a tribute to the variety and vividness of Portugal's people, above all Pessoa.

The narrator soon realizes that the appointment for twelve o'clock must not have been for noon but for midnight, and he spends the intervening hours in his successive encounters with people who are listed at the front of the book in the same way that places are listed in *Nocturne*. As in *Nocturne*, there are odd gaps in continuity. For instance, the most moving encounter is that with Isabel (she returns in other work by Tabucchi), a former lover who has killed herself for reasons that the narrator has never fully understood. When her presence is announced in an adjoining room of the decrepit club where the narrator is playing billiards, he walks toward the room—and the scene shifts to another location, another encounter, with no indication of what the narrator found out and with what emotions. The last encounter is with The Poet, who is clearly Pessoa; the two writers dine in an upscale restaurant, putting the older writer face-to-face with the postmodernism that he helped to bring about and which, it seems, he does not much like. Whatever imperatives were being played out in this series of hallucinated encounters have now, it seems, been fulfilled. For in a brief and simple closing, the narrator finds himself once more in a darkening garden in Azeitão, beneath a mulberry tree, stretched out in a deck chair with a book on his lap.

THE SUBDRAMA OF WRITING

If the interpenetration of dreaming and waking realms is a subject for Pessoa's writing, it may also be characteristic of writing itself, according to Bernardo Soares:

> And so, many times, I write without wanting to think, in an external daydreaming, allowing the words to play around me, as if I were a little girl hanging on their necks. They are sentences without meaning, softly flowing, in a fluidity of felt water, a forgetting oneself on the shore where the waves mix and lose definition, always becom-

ing others, succeeding each other. In the same way, ideas, images, tremulous with expression, pass through me in sonorous corteges like silk dyed in varied shades, where the moonlight of ideas spins, whirling and confused. (9)

This heady evocation is reminiscent of the metamorphoses of hypnagogia—compare the wave imagery here to that of de Chirico in *Hebdomeros*—and arises out of a similar liminal state. One thinks again of Borges's comment that writing is nothing more than a guided dream (20). Still, in that formulation there is an author who guides the dream. Here, it is the dream that is guiding—that is, in a sense, doing the writing. Agency is absent, and for Pessoa "forgetting oneself" on the shore of this sea of dreams is a relief. The burden of selfhood, as it has been described in "The Forest of Alienation," is to some degree lifted in the act of writing. But only to some degree. The residue of self-consciousness can be dispelled only by writing as *other*, indeed as many others; the arrival of the heteronyms in Pessoa's life responds to this need. These heteronyms produce a writing that is a dreaming-as-other. Indeed, as I have noted, dreaming itself is always done as other, it is a writing of which we are not the authors. Within the parenthesis of night, it authors *us*. "If I dream, it seems I'm being written," Soares tells us (146).

Writing as dream, dream as writing: the interpenetrations are complex and restless. Restlessness in particular, Herschel Farbman has pointed out in his subtle and wide-ranging *The Other Night*, is a characteristic of this liminal state, one that has often been referenced in the writing that has emerged from it. Yet the elusiveness of this state makes it an extraordinarily difficult subject to deal with in anything more than momentary glimpses. Blanchot, writing in a necessarily elliptical mode, has repeatedly essayed to bring this state, and its implications, into our awareness. He does this as a philosopher; his novels take other directions, not unrelated ones. But perhaps the only novel that fully takes on this state as its central concern and challenge is one written by Philippe Sollers; it has intrigued and baffled critics since its appearance in 1965.

The disequilibrium into which Sollers's *Drame: Roman* throws its readers begins with the genre tensions of its title.[8] On the novel's back cover, though, Sollers provides an explanation that is nowhere found inside the covers: "The word *drama* is here meant in its oldest sense, not that of action—even less psychological plot—but rather that of 'story,' 'event.'"[9] *Event*, indeed, is the title chosen by the translators of the English version. But what exactly is this event? It is not really equivalent to "story" and even less equivalent to the events recounted in this story, for there are none—at least none of the kind that we usually expect. Rather, the event is the act of writing itself, quite apart from anything written. What we are given is what the narrator of *Event* hypothesizes: "a suspended story in which nothing would ever seem to happen, but which would be the epitome of an inner activity" (35).[10] The story here, as Roland Barthes has observed, is "the desire for the story" ("Event" 93), and the inner activity of which Sollers is speaking is one that both initiates that desire and strives to fulfill it. *Event* is a book about the inception of a book—not as in Proust or Wordsworth, where the events are those of an autobiography and its accompanying revelations, eventually bringing the writer to the point where he knows what his great work must be about and is ready to begin writing it. In *Event* writing is not a matter of "communicating" an already decided-upon subject matter, but an altogether more complex thing, which must now become the novel's explicit subject, as it was always its implicit one:

> Writing takes place in and must pass into the ground *[fond]* of all forms, including those it activates as it writes itself; it must tell what it does even as it does it. The novel we have in mind would be one that opens itself fully to this inexhaustible possibility, a possibility continually decentered and annulled, that can never be fixed in this or that particular story. (200)

This is Sollers giving a lecture titled "The Novel and the Experience of Limits" in 1965, the same year in which *Drame* was published. "The novel we have in mind" would then be his own.

Event (as I will now continue to refer to it) begins with a beginning, with a writer ready to write: "Starting" *(D'abord)* is the novel's first word and its prolonged action. The premise that this moment of beginning "may be the stablest element that clusters behind the eyes and forehead" is quickly undercut as the writer becomes aware of images and impulses within his entire body and realizes that "there is no way to begin with the necessary guarantees of neutrality" (1; repeated on 26). Any beginning has always already begun. Moreover, for this writer, it begins interminably: the book that he is writing never emerges from these pages, except as a book about writing, "continually decentered and annulled."

The book alternates between sections describing a state of mind in a nameless third-person "him" and sections preceded by the words "He writes." The latter do not—as one might expect—give us writing that is the product of the preceding state of mind. Rather, they describe, now using the first person, a state of mind that "I" holds, or is held by. This alternation between "I" and "him" is reminiscent of Sollers's observation about what happens within the space of literature opened by Mallarmé: "The same and the other speak themselves together *[se disent ensemble]*; when the same speaks, the other falls silent—but this silence remains an active and accentuated speech. The fiction is *confirmed,* or in other words continually written and played out at its source" ("Literature and Totality" 79). This continual writing, we come to understand, is a *mental* one. It need not be related to actual writing, need not be only something that takes place before a page that is being filled. It is also the way in which the physical world that the writer inhabits—a port city, with its heavy machinery, seabirds, winding streets, facades, municipal gardens—is made to come into being. That process might be called a kind of reading, the interpretation of signs in the world that are already there. However, for Sollers (returning to his comments on Mallarmé), "Scriptor and reader are situated on the same side of the fictive screen; their operations become simultaneous and complementary" (79).

There is also a "you" that inhabits the pages of this novel, and that has various and overlapping meanings: (1) "You" is the narrator's lover; she is both described and addressed—that is to say, she is being read and is herself the reader of this work. (2) She thus stands in for and can be identified with any reader of Sollers's novel, a reader who is also being both described and addressed:

> You move forward with me in this story, and you surprise me, the
> way you take the turns of this imperceptible journey, hour after hour,
> day after day, seemingly without losing anything of a dull intensity,

a certainty you find outside of me, zone of shadow and spontaneity
(you act as if you can see beyond you, really see something, as if you
are the property of something whose secret orders you follow), unfo-
cused zone behind your face that seems as if it is asleep in a distant
perpetual absorption, aside from brief nervous breakthroughs, high
points to which it's impossible to make you return. (25)

This is a unique description of reading viewed from the outside as
a peculiar sort of trance—though as the passage continues it turns
smoothly into a description of a woman's face in a train. And "you" is
both of these, and more. Since "you" is what Sollers is writing about
in the passage, "you" is also the subject of his novel, in more than
one sense: if scriptor and reader are indeed on the same side of the
fictive screen, "you" can also be "him"—and both are fictive. At one
point, for instance, the description of a marine scene as night falls
moves seamlessly from what is before the narrator's eyes to what is
behind them:

He is in the night that he is. He holds a kind of reduced version of
it, under his eyes—but he has himself disappeared in it (he realizes,
in other words, that there is no "subject"—no more than on this
page). (62)

The dissolution of one version of "you" into another culminates,
then, in the dissolution of any subject position from which "you" can
be viewed. This includes both the subject that is the author's self and
the subject that is the matter of his novel.

If this is a novel without a subject, that doesn't mean that it is
not "about" something; for, as has already been said, it deals with an
event, a certain inner activity that precedes writing and may be said
as well to precede a coherent self. It describes a process that precedes
the conscious start of a book. Not that this process takes place within
something that we might comfortably christen "the unconscious."
Rather, the writer describes himself as inhabiting a *liminal* space:
"I feel as if I am at the edge of words, just before they can be seen
or heard, near a book dreaming itself with infinite patience" (43). If
this is his state "just before" the advent of words, it is perhaps not
that different from his state just "after": "He regains consciousness,

here at the edge, after having sunk for an instant in full daylight into what he does not know" (50). Both states are on an edge, and the words the writer brings back are hardly free of the vagueness that preceded them: "He is holding on to something as if through a thick static *[brouillage intense]*, from the start" (50). What he has brought back in the form of words—however tentative—has edges of its own, which continually threaten to dissolve words back into the space from which they emerged. When for once he has achieved "a preserved, emphasized sentence" it is also one "above and beneath which countless associations were being unleashed" (64). For, he realizes, "each word lives at its own periphery" (71). And that is the problem for both writer and reader: "how to follow the urgings, the appeals, the slants of quick visions ('fern' is also the presence of the hidden sun, a carpet of luminous spots where all autumns are imprinted)" (44).

Those "quick visions" partake of both the obbligato effect and hypnagogic imagery. Roland Barthes cites a passage in *L'Intermediaire* dedicated to catnaps in order to support his argument that Sollers's writing practice is a liminal one. The passage is not particularly convincing as evidence of this, but the argument is:

> In his writing, sleep and the waking state are . . . terms of a formal
> function: sleep is the figure of *before*, the waking state the figure of
> *after*, and awakening is the neutral moment when their opposition
> can be perceived, expressed; sleep is essentially anterior, the scene
> of the indivisible beginning. ("Event" 97)

The argument is convincing because its terms occur repeatedly in *Event*, whose narrator is continually described as waking, sometimes literally, sometimes figuratively. At such moments it is not so much an opposition that is being expressed as a transition. For instance: "Surprise of waking up, this time. . . . Eyes closed, it shifts, tilts, begins to spin, briefly bringing back unforeseeable fragments (it's a matter of a movement that he can't endow with speech)" (68). Or he speaks of "waking up on the inside of sleep" (64)—a peculiar phrase, and one that may be best explicated by a passage occurring a few pages before, where he is in the process of returning "cautiously" from a dream, bringing it back with him:

But that is when the accident occurs: black flash, collision in the unregulated fringe where I am half asleep . . . a silent blasting in my temples, my cheeks, and once again my eyes are open. . . . That's when there is a limitless lucidity, the room as screen dissolves, it loses its closed aspect, city, country, period, makeshift and hidden box—it radiates beyond me, everything begins to wake up, to be punctuated by waves, in sheets (which depends on the eyes and the inside of the eyes in a vibrating medium that seems as if it is beyond air). It is all at once an upheaval and a spawning living in a curtain of atoms, of blue points. (60)

This last vision can be linked to Levinas's "swarming of points": both describe a physical phenomenon with metaphysical implications. Here Sollers awakens into a kind of double exposure, partaking simultaneously of the eyes and the "inside of the eyes." When "everything begins to wake up," then, it is not into the lucidity of rational order, but into another sort of lucidity altogether—one that always underlies our usual patterns of perception but is so hidden by habit that we cannot "see" it, either in the physical or the cognitive sense of that word. Here it is seen during a moment of waking, but it may be seen as well at the opposite border of sleep. The narrator speaks of "seeing again before sleep certain episodes of the gravity pulling on us (confused, fluid recollection that is already the same as the other side of sleep)" (48). This "gravity" may be the heaviness of oncoming sleep; but it may also be a pull toward a realm that we remain unaware of in our waking life, preferring to call "life" whatever emerges into our conscious categories of control: Sollers's writer refers to "the edge of the margin from which we emerge for a few moments (life)" (71). What we call life is parenthetically embedded in a larger, more marginal realm, which we feel compelled to resist, dismiss, or explain away. Yet, when that resistance slackens, when we yield to the pull of that dark gravity, its heaviness disappears and we find ourselves in what might truly be called the unbearable lightness of being: "All heaviness disappears, a sort of intoxication signals the beginning of drift, and this is perhaps what happens during that nocturnal gliding—whispery, silken grazings—slope of the game where you have to end up, dizziness, a brief disappearance" (34). Yielding to the gravity of sleep can produce this effect, but it can also be produced by a *sentence,* which is in fact what has produced the effect that Sollers's writer describes here. The drift *[dérive]* recalls Barthes's use of the same word in *The Pleasure of the Text* to describe the state of being "driven about by language's illusions, seductions, and intimidations, like a cork on the waves" (18). So the next section of Sollers's novel picks up on this phantasmatic event by way of its inadequate representation in words: "Poorly mimicked images in which he rediscovers the game near sleep (this time he stays on the edge)" (34). The "game" appears to be one of finding exactly the notch in which hypnagogic images manifest themselves, to be represented later in words.

Sollers's novel is then a study of what has traditionally been called "inspiration," though it turns that tradition on its head. His predecessor in this is Maurice Blanchot, who describes inspiration as a "nocturnal state" (*Space* 182). Sollers too (or his stand-in), near the conclusion of his novel, writes, "For the first time, I understand the rapport that unites what I write with the night" (82). And as he continues to write, he observes, parenthetically, "I am writing into the night."

EXPERIMENT, EXPERIENCE

So far as I know, Sollers's novel has escaped the label "experimental fiction"—so far. That label is vague at best, misleading at worst, a way of relegating to the margins of literature anything that does not conform to the conventions of realism; it has been applied even to such canonical texts as *Ulysses* (Lawrence 3–15). One can only imagine what Joyce would have had to say about this, about the implication that he was just trying something out to see if it would work before settling down to write a real novel. In a trenchant article defending "experimental" fiction, Ben Marcus points out that the term itself is complicit with a certain dismissiveness:

> Calling a writer experimental is now the equivalent of saying his work does not matter, is not readable, and is aggressively masturbatory. But why is it an experiment to attempt something artistic? A painter striving for originality is not called experimental. (42)

Writers who have been labeled "experimental" in fact have a very good idea of what they are doing and why they are doing it, as I hope to show later with the help of statements from the writers themselves. The experiment, if there is one, is more on the part of readers, who have to adjust their familiar expectations of what it means to read; but even this could better be described not as an experiment but as an experience. This wider term avoids the provisional, marginal connotations of an experiment, and at the same time it comprehends the experimental as an element of anything that could be isolated as an experience, as opposed to daily routines. Such routines are comforting or boring as the case may be, but they are always characterized by being entirely predictable. They may "be experienced," passively, but they are not "an experience." An experience stands out because it is unpredictable, because it introduces a new element that must be reacted to in new ways; it thus includes, always, an element of the experimental. And if our experiences count for more in our lives than our daily routines, this means that the experimental element is not something that can be indulged in at the margins until the experiment is deemed to be successful, at which time it is admitted to the circle of things that count. Rather, what counts as experience is always experimental; it disquiets us, sometimes pleasurably, but always in a way that demands that we rethink our usual modes of being.

In literature, experience disquiets us, often, in ways that lead back to the liminal. So Blanchot can write:

> The work tends ever increasingly to manifest the experience of the work: the experience which is not exactly that of its creation and which is not that of its technical fashioning either. The experience leads the work ceaselessly back from the clarity of the beginning to the obscurity of the origin. (*Space* 204)

That obscurity must always be profoundly unsettling. But we recall that for Blanchot it is the business of literature to unsettle us, to bring us from the daylight world of clear and articulated meanings to one where "nothing has meaning yet, toward which nevertheless everything which does have meaning returns as toward its origin" (*Space* 196). For Foucault, too, this is the receding point toward which literature today must continually move. As he states in his essay "Language to Infinity":

> Writing, in our day, has moved infinitely closer to its sources, to this disquieting sound which announces from the depths of language— once we attend to it—the source against which we seek refuge and toward which we address ourselves. . . . We must ceaselessly speak, for as long and as loudly as this indefinite and deafening noise—longer and more loudly so that in mixing our voices with it we might succeed—if not in silencing and mastering it—in modulating its futility into the endless murmuring we call literature. (60)

Foucault has clearly borrowed from Blanchot's writings this description of literature as murmuring, inarticulate, and inarticulable (e.g., *Space* 48). And in this 1963 essay, originally published in *Tel Quel*, he might well have been thinking of work by Sollers, editor of the journal and the subject of an essay by Foucault in that same year; *Drame* appeared two years later.

Writing in our day continues the tendency that Foucault noted in his, with a number of so-called experimental writers associating their work with liminal states. Among these is Laird Hunt, whose 2009 *Ray of the Star* has a title that is apparently without any relation to the contents of that novel. The title is in fact derived from a meditation by Blanchot on the mutual permeability of day and night. It begins:

> Lucidity, ray of the star, response to the day that questions, and sleep when night comes. "But who will hide from the star that never sets?" Wakefulness is without beginning or end. To wake is neutral. "I" do not wake; someone does, the night does, always and incessantly, hollowing the night out into the other night where there can be no question of sleeping. (*Disaster* 48)[11]

To convey this incessant hollowing out of daylight wakefulness, Hunt writes each of his brief chapters in a single long sentence, the convolutions of which range freely from the actions being performed at the moment to the obbligato of memories and associations that accompany them, and that to some degree determine them. Here is an example from early in *Ray of the Star*:

Leave, Harry thought so he locked the front door, threw the keys into the snarled forsythia, got into his car and drove past houses he had long ago stopped looking at and did not look at now, and knew he would never look at again, and then they were behind him and the country beside the highway opened up, when there weren't any subdivisions or industrial parks, onto cow-peppered grassland above which hawks circled and balloons hung heavily and gliders scraped away at the sky, an endless, hopeless affair the color of a postcard he had been sent, unsigned, some years earlier from a great city where he had once spent a few happy months, some kind of blue with a few drops of bloody red in it, which called to mind a drink he had once had but couldn't remember the composition of as he had sat in a bar in that great city and smashed himself to smithereens for no compelling reason, the way he had done many things in that particular part of his deep past, when he had worked hardly at all and slept a great deal and very little had mattered, much like, he thought as he took the exit for the airport, now, this moment, these last years, although the situations were not the same, oh no, even if very little now mattered and very little had mattered then there had been those intervening years when everything had mattered and that changed it, irrevocably, and as he walked away from his car, he thought again of the great city and that shade of blue, which had surely shifted over the years he had kept the postcard—part of a collection which even now, as he set his credit card down on the counter and said the name of the great city, was sitting, continuing to shift, in an Adidas box beside his desk in the house that years ago had stopped being his home. (3–4)

Even before this passage begins its embedded associations of the sky to the color of a postcard to the color of a drink, there is something disconcerting in the seamless transitions from front door to car to neighboring houses to subdivisions and industrial parks to grasslands. That these transitions are not implicitly categorized in separate sentences foregrounds the uncanniness of time, the way that it includes in its unbroken flow the most diverse atmospheres and events. To find a center to changes that one can observe even in such an ordinary activity as a trip to the airport—if we suspend for a moment the dulling effect of custom—is a task as great as that posed by insomnia's restless circlings. This sentence, always on the verge of flying apart, is like Harry surely seeking some sort of lucidity. What it finds or what we are given instead is only a series of shiftings from one association to another, and one change in time following another, returning at the end to a postcard in a drawer inside the house that Harry left at the beginning of the sentence, a postcard that has shifted in time and is continuing to shift. This insomniac movement evokes Blanchot's other night, "where there can be no question of sleeping," and it does so in the midst of Harry's waking day. The effect is deliberate: Hunt has asserted that the liminal is tremendously important for his work, though his novels may evoke it in different ways. In *Ray of the Star*, he says, "the natural result of the single sentence mechanism was a language field constantly torquing away from waking state into dream state."[12]

Another example of the experimental revealing itself as liminal is Aaron Kunin's novel *The Mandarin*. The author's synopsis preceding the text tells us that "the entire novel takes place on the border between sleep and waking" (i). This is so because "the characters are constantly falling asleep, trying to fall asleep, or trying to wake up." Yet this motif appears only at intervals, and the liminal quality of the novel, as with Hunt's, has more to do with its techniques. Foremost among these is the fact that the novel is written almost entirely in dialogue—which is not to say that the characters are necessarily talking *to* one another. Rather, Kunin has borrowed Virginia Woolf's format in *The Waves*, where the repeated tag "he said" or "she said" introduces not an actual utterance but a person's state of mind at the moment (Lerner). In Kunin's novel, though, "consciousness tends to be communal rather than personal" (iii), and this is so to an extraordinary degree. At one point two characters, Hallamore and Willy, fall asleep in the same bed; when they awake, "their memories are momentarily confused"—not confused as Proust is disoriented upon waking, but confused in a mix-up of memories. Kunin has explained that he is here playing on a scenario by William James:

> The first principle in James's psychology is that consciousness is personal. My thoughts are my thoughts, and no one else's; I can

describe my thoughts to other people, but I can't give the experience of my thoughts to another person. James's beautiful example is a scene where two men, Peter and Paul, fall asleep next to each other and then wake up together. In the moment of waking, James says, each man adheres to his own consciousness. There is no possibility of an exchange between consciousnesses; Peter can't wake up with Paul's memories, ideas, and associations in his head, or be mistaken about which memories are his [*Psychology* 1:238–39]. Such exchanges are the rule in *The Mandarin*. When Willy and Hallamore wake up next to each other, they reconstruct their consciousnesses with whatever is handy, and each one picks up something that used to belong to the other.[13]

Similarly, in a sequence of "he said" and "she said" that is more a series of mental moments than an articulated communication, a statement by one character may nevertheless be picked up by others. So it is that, in the words of the synopsis, "the plot develops recursively rather than progressively as a kind of theme-and-variations" (i). Even this explanation is misleading, since in theme-and-variations the variations are always anchored by the theme, and implicitly related to it. In *The Mandarin* the variations may gradually bend the theme through a series of tangential variations so that it becomes something quite different from what it was when it started. This movement has certain affinities, perhaps, with Dennett's multiple-draft theory, according to which consciousness is only "something like a narrative stream or sequence" because it is constantly darting off to other associative possibilities, if only provisionally. Or the movement of variations might be related to Blanchot's "resemblances"—encompassing both similarity and difference—which are a dynamic of dream though not confined to dream. Finally, these variations may be a consciously rendered version of an obbligato effect that is usually an unconscious accompaniment to reading. Something like this seems to be implied near the end of the novel when the narrator, Willy, speaks of an operation on one eye that has rather peculiarly affected his ability to read:

> Because the eye that had been operated on had never healed satisfactorily, it could not absorb words very easily; it could only release

them. One eye was always releasing words while the other was trying to absorb them, so that I could not distinguish, when I had a
book in front of me, between the words that were on the page, offering themselves up for inspection, and the words that were pouring
out of my eye and crowding the others out. (178–79)

The words of *The Mandarin* simultaneously offer themselves up for
inspection (in a lean, energetic idiom) and convey a crowd of darting
associations. The text operates, as it were, on the reader's eye, making it difficult to distinguish between form and fantasm, daylight
and night vision. Kunin's accomplishment could then be described,
with no disrespect, in the same words that are applied to all of Willy's
novels: "He pretends that he is a writer or that he has written something, but obviously he isn't writing novels, he's producing a more
potent sleep-inducing object" (58). Of course according to the narrator of *The Arabian Nightmare* this is what a novel *should* be: if it does
not actually put us to sleep, it should bring us close to the threshold,
and should most properly be read in bed.

> "I've written a novel by night," I said. "*To Be Read by Night, a novel*. I
> did it on slices of bread that glow with a rose-colored light for you to
> read it by." (*Mandarin* 169)

"I" is Willy; "Willy" is William Kunin (177); however, William
Kunin's initials are AK: "'I'm not a very literary outcast after all,' I
said, 'but I do have the same initials as Alfred Kazin'" (118). So while
Willy writes many novels in the course of *The Mandarin*, as evanescent as they are easy (he writes one in the steam that has condensed
on a window), this last one may well refer to the novel we have been
reading. Funny, often bewildering, always thought-provoking, *The
Mandarin* is, as they say, the best thing since sliced bread.

   Or since Raymond Queneau, whose work can often be described
in the same terms. Queneau's 1965 novel *Les Fleurs bleues* brings us
back to the problem of the philosopher and the butterfly with which
this section began: its Greek epigraph, from Plato's *Theaetetus*, may
be translated as "a dream for a dream." The novel involves a peculiar
dream exchange. It opens in the twelfth century with the Duke of
Auge considering "the historical situation" from the height of his

castle keep; but as soon as he falls asleep he dreams that he is called Cidrolin and is living on a barge christened *The Ark,* moored near a twentieth-century metropolis. Cidrolin has peculiar dreams—for instance, that he lives in the Middle Ages—and they seem moreover to be continuous. When he takes his nap after lunch he is once again on his way to see how the building of Notre Dame Cathedral is getting on. So it continues, with Cidrolin and the Duke of Auge waking into each other's lives every time they fall asleep. At intervals, however, the Duke of Auge skips over 175 years, until he finally appears before Cidrolin's barge and moves in, along with his entourage. After setting straight certain problems in Cidrolin's life, he cuts the mooring rope and *The Ark* begins to move on the river. The river swells to a flood under a steady downpour of rain, and the barge drifts until it runs aground on a castle keep. Refreshed by a good night's sleep, the Duke goes over to the battlements to consider the historical situation.

Much of the criticism of *Les Fleurs bleues* has gone along with the Duke in considering the historical situation, or the situation of history itself, as it is playfully implied in this work. They have a certain warrant for doing so in a work that Queneau published the following year, *Une Histoire modéle.* Begun in 1942 and left unfinished, this work was belatedly published by Queneau because, among other reasons, it seemed to him that it might be useful to readers of *Les Fleurs bleues* (*Histoire* 8). But Queneau has also cited, in connection with *Les Fleurs bleues,* Zhuangzi's dream of a butterfly dreaming him (Knapp 46). The inability to compartmentalize dreaming and waking worlds is also the subject of "Dream Accounts Aplenty," one of the pieces in Queneau's *Stories and Remarks.* There are fifteen short, off-kilter accounts in this piece; only at the end are we told:

> *Of course none of these dreams are any more real than they are invented. They are simply minor incidents taken from wakened life. A minimal effort of rhetoric seemed sufficient to give them a dreamlike aspect.*
> *That's all I wanted to say.* (137)

What he is saying here has also been said by others in his circle— Michel Leiris for one, who provided a preface to *Stories and Remarks.* Leiris too collected a series of dream accounts, but interspersed these with other accounts, labeled *"real-life"* and sometimes *"half-asleep"* or *"daytime fantasy."* The tacit invitation is to consider whether there really is all that much difference between these incidents, whether waking or dreamed, or somewhere between. Richard Sieburth, who translated this book under the title *Nights as Day, Days as Night,* has commented on the original title as follows: *"Nuits sans nuit et quelques jours sans jour* pursues an extended pun on the porous demarcation between waking and dreaming. A literal translation of its title would read: Nights without night and several days without day" (xv). What the contents of this book are "without" are the clear categories of night and day, which in Leiris's juxtapositions reveal themselves to be more "porous" than we might have thought.

It is André Breton, though, who provides the most explicit and extended consideration of this porosity. To be sure, his metaphor is a different one: *Communicating Vessels,* he calls his 1955 treatise. Mary Ann Caws, one of the book's translators, explains the reference:

> The title image of "communicating vessels" is taken from a scientific experiment of the same name: in vessels joined by a tube, a gas or liquid passing from one to the other rises to the same level in each, whatever the form of the vessel. This passing back and forth between two modes is shown to be the basis of Surrealist thought, of Surreality itself.
>
> Personifying these modes are the two imagined figures of sleep and wakefulness. . . . They represent the communicating vessels of interior vision and exterior fact, of night and day, "unreal" and "real." (ix)

It is important to stress that communicating is not the same thing as equating. Breton has the same scorn as Lacan does for the easy formula *Life is a dream (Four Fundamental Concepts* 53, 55). For if—like the Chinese philosopher—we believe ourselves to be awake while we are asleep, we do not correspondingly believe ourselves to be asleep while we are awake: "Why this cheating in favor of sleep?" Breton asks (107). He then offers a subtler argument for the communication between the dream and the waking world. After describing an extended erotic fantasy that accompanied him throughout his day,

Breton links it to the dream state and then extends this particular observation to a more general one: that the waking world, like the dream world, is traversed by desire; all else is dimmed by habit or relegated to the periphery of our awareness. This does not mean that desire negates the waking or material world:

> Desire, if it is truly vital, refuses itself nothing. However, even if it finds the raw material it uses indifferent up to a certain point, it is not so richly inclined as to the manner of treating it. Whether in reality or in the dream, it is constrained, in fact, to make the elements pass through the same network: condensation, displacement, substitutions, alterations. (109)

So Breton can speak of "the state of waking dream, where the greatest part of the waking attention functions" (111). Attention, which is sometimes made the touchstone of the waking state, is here revealed as directed and distorted by our desires rather than by the material world in all its fullness. That world has a concrete existence, but our *experience* of it is no more precise than that of our dream experiences. For the most part it is a faint impression at the edges of our consciousness.

Breton at one point compares this liminality that characterizes most of the outside world, as it is actually experienced by us, to the liminal nature of a literary world, of the world as it is depicted in the most conventionally realistic literature. Breton has already spoken of one component of his waking day, the Café Batifol, and now returns to it in this new, liminal light:

> The Café Batifol is no myth; you could even make one of those naturalistic descriptions of it whose completely photographic graciousness does not exclude a very faint exterior objective resemblance. (I love those descriptions: you are there and not there; there are, it seems, so many aspidistras on the false marble counter not completely white and green; in the evening lamplight, a lace pattern of dew, seen from one angle, links the necklines of blouses, where there always dangles as far as the eye can reach the same little rhinestone crucifix, meant to heighten the sparkle of the rouge and the mascara, and so on. All of that is not completely devoid of interest, moreover; we arrive, in this way, at total imprecision.) (104–5)

The parenthetical aside does two things at once. In a prose not devoid of surrealist touches ("a lace pattern of dew . . . links the necklines of blouses") Breton presents an alternative to that "naturalistic description" that is itself linked to photographic documentation. Breton's brief description of the Café Batifol leaves out most of the thorough itemization that objectivity requires, in favor of a few impressions traversed by desire in its most recognizable form (those necklines again). He gives us, in short, a precise description of the imprecision of actual experience. At the same time, he reminds us that even (or perhaps especially) in the most painstaking itemization of the material world, the outcome is never the material world but something else. Indeed the closer the description comes to an "exterior objective resemblance" the more we sense that it is and can only ever be "very faint." If Breton—rather unexpectedly for a surrealist—loves naturalistic descriptions, it is likely because their claims to accuracy, taken to the extreme, only succeed in bringing out the strangeness of literary description as such—all the ways in which "you are there and not there." The naturalistic description, quite against its intentions, ends up providing an experience that is not so different from that provided by Breton's impressionistic description; the descriptions may be thought of as communicating vessels, for their contents level out at the same degree of liminality, regardless of what the vessel's shape may be.

Yet Breton, in providing us with his description of the Café Batifol, is implicitly making a claim that his version is more true to the reality of experience; the only difference is that the naturalistic description is liminal in spite of itself. Marcus makes a similar appeal to an experiential reality beyond the conventions of realism, an appeal that is mistrusted by another "experimental" novelist, Brian Evenson. "To suggest that experimental fiction represents a different reality," Evenson says, "prioritizes the notion of reality, which in turn prioritizes mimetic literature, which in turn lets realism control the argument" (325). Of course not every realism is equivalent to every other, with the same "real" being represented. "The novel, in a sense, cannot escape realism, for language too is *a* reality"—this is yet another "experimental" novelist, Raymond Federman, in an essay provocatively titled "What Are Experimental Novels and Why Are There So Many Left Unread?" (30). Writing fourteen years before Marcus's article, Federman might almost be responding directly to Marcus's argument:

> Can it be said that by denouncing the fraudulence of a "usual" novel which tends to totalize existence and misses its pluridimensionality the experimental work in a way frees us from the illusion of realism?
>
> I rather believe that it encloses us in it. Because the goal remains the same: it is always a question of expressing, of translating something which is already there—even if to be already there, in this new perspective, consists paradoxically in not being there. . . .
>
> However, let's not kid ourselves, reality as such has never really interested anyone; it is and always has been a form of disenchantment. What makes reality fascinating at times is the imaginary catastrophe which hides behind it. The writer knows this and exploits it. (29–30)

Federman's vague term "imaginary catastrophe" might be related to Blanchot's "disaster"—and consequently to that "endless murmuring" of which Foucault speaks, and which he identifies with literature itself. This connection may not have been intended by Federman, but it is one that is attuned to his position. That position is a liminal one: the writer translates something that is already there and at the same time is not there. Like murmuring, literature (articulately) promises a full articulation that it never reaches, cannot possibly reach. Its necessary shortfall is a disaster that continually sends readers back to a realm that precedes language, out of which language arises. It is the turn back to an unknowable realm, incessantly in motion, that paradoxically marks literature's success—success as a failure that is *aware*. So, in Blanchot's reworking of the myth, Orpheus turns around at the last moment of his journey out of the underworld not as a fatal mistake but *in order* to send Eurydice back to the shades. The work is there in order to become not-there—which is not to give absence the priority, for the work's "resonant disappearance," in Mallarmé's phrase (368),[14] depends upon its having previously appeared. We have a version, then, of Breton's "communicating vessels," an experiment that acquires its significance for him not because the contents of these vessels attain the same level, but because of their continual passings back and forth. In Breton's version, the "experiment" is never concluded or conclusive, yielding a piece of significant information that can then be classified among the things we know. Rather, we inhabit endlessly, ceaselessly, interminably— these are Blanchot's repeated terms—a realm in which "there is no meaning yet" but in which meaning is in the interminable process of becoming. This is a liminal zone: there and not there, real and unreal, day vision and night vision. It is the zone that literature necessarily inhabits. And it may be literature's most profound function to remind us that this is also the zone that we must necessarily inhabit.

ACKNOWLEDGMENTS

Nobody writes alone, not even in the dead of night, and I have profited enormously from people who have helped me think about the dim and liminal realm to which these pages are devoted. The bibliography at the end of this book indicates something of its intellectual debt, but I would like here to single out a number of people for the personal generosity that in the academy goes by "collegiality." Always more than merely being nice, collegiality is to my mind largely made up of the capacity to be curious and enthusiastic about work that may be miles away from one's own interests, and to contribute whatever one can to the accomplishment of that work.

I thank Kevin Davis for his rich and thoughtful master's thesis, "Hypnogony: The Sleep of Philosophy—An Art of Sleep"; Rob Switzer for the disconcerting insights of his as-yet unpublished paper "The Sleep of Reason: Phenomenology and Its Shadow"; Eric Savoy for putting me on to "Harvey's Dream"; Simon van Rysewyk for pinpointing a quotation from Wittgenstein; D. M. Bentley for sending a quotation from Agamben; Graham Fraser for introducing me to the novels of Laird Hunt; Laird Hunt and Aaron Kunin for answering impertinent questions about their work; Tony Purdy and Brian Stimpson for helping me find my way in the great continent of writing by Valéry (though they are not responsible, of course, for what I then did with or to him); J. Keeping for his balanced critique of my paper "The Melancholy of Waking"; Hugo Moreno for talking with me about Pessoa over coffee; Laurence Bush for a tip about sleepwalking; and Inga Roemer and Colette Beck for engaged conversation.

This project was supported by two grants from the Social Sciences and Humanities Research Council of Canada. These grants paid for the invaluable assistance of two exemplary research assistants, Madeline Bassnett and Jeremy Greenway.

I am grateful to the Department of English and the Centre for the Study of Theory and Criticism at the University of Western Ontario; they made the move to a strange city seem like a homecoming.

Finally, once again, Steven Bruhm—for countless recommendations and resistances, and for doing what he can to keep me awake.

NOTES

PREFACE

1. "Identity and Trembling," 13; and again in *The Fall of Sleep*, 13: "There is no phenomenology of sleep." But for one piece of a possible phenomenology, see Jan Linschoten, "On Falling Asleep." And see the fine paper, as yet unpublished, by Robert Switzer (switzer@aucegypt.edu): "The Sleep of Reason: Phenomenology and Its Shadow."

2. "How often has it happened to me that in the night I dreamt that I found myself in this particular place, that I was dressed and seated near the fire, whilst in reality I was lying undressed in bed! At this moment it does indeed seem to me that it is with eyes awake that I am looking at this paper; that this head which I move is not asleep, that it is deliberately and of set purpose that I extend my hand and perceive it; what happens in sleep does not appear so clear nor so distinct as does all this. But in thinking over this I remind myself that on many occasions I have in sleep been deceived by similar illusions, and in dwelling carefully on this reflection I see so manifestly that there are no certain indications by which we may clearly distinguish wakefulness from sleep that I am lost in astonishment. And my astonishment is such that it is almost capable of persuading me that I now dream" (13). Another version of the conundrum will be picked up in the last section of this book.

3. I have used Richard Sieburth's translation of the preface to Michel Leiris's *Nights as Day, Days as Night*. The essay is more readily available in Blanchot's *Friendship*, translated by Elizabeth Rottenberg, but I have found that Sieburth's translation brings out my point better.

I. TOWARD SLEEP

1. I owe this reference as well as the opening quotation from Merleau-Ponty to Kevin Davis's "Hypnogony."

2. Reports from informants in Mavromatis's *Hypnagogia* have provided the elements of this description. It can only be "fairly" representative because there are less common versions of hypnagogia that are verbal rather than imagistic (as reported by André Breton in the quotation given in note 4), or even olfactory and tactile. There is also the related phenomenon of hypnopompic imagery, which takes place at the other end of sleep: upon waking one continues to see, distinctly, images from a preceding dream.

3. On Hawthorne, see Susan Katherine Hopkins Kurijaka's 1992 dissertation "'Waking Dream': Hawthorne's Hypnagogic Image of the Imagination." On Wolf, see Andrew Winnard, "'These Drowsy Approaches of Sleep': Christa Wolf and the Hypnagogic Dream." See also my own study of Christa Wolf and hypnagogia in *Fantasm and Fiction*, 37–46.

4. "It was in 1919, in complete solitude and at the approach of sleep, that my attention was arrested by sentences, more or less complete, which became perceptible to my mind without my being able to discover (even by meticulous analysis) any possible previous volitional effort. One evening in particular, as I was about to fall asleep, I became aware of a sentence articulated clearly to a point excluding all possibility of alteration and stripped of all quality of vocal sound. . . . I am unable at this distance to remember the exact sentence, but it ran something like this: 'A man is cut in half by the window.' What made it clearer was the fact that it was accompanied by a feeble visual representation of a man in the process of walking, but cloven, at half his height, by a window perpendicular to the axis of his body. Definitely, there was the form, re-erected against space, of a man leaning out of a window. But, with the window following the man's locomotion, I understood that I was dealing with an image of great rarity. Instantly the idea came to me to use it as material for poetic construction" (*What Is Surrealism?* 120).

This account follows the general pattern of hypnagogic experiences, but it differs in that the visual representation is "feeble" in contrast to the focused and articulated nature of most hypnagogic imagery. The auditory component that begins the experience, too, is "stripped of all quality of vocal sound"—a phenomenon more characteristic of dream communications than of hypnagogic ones.

5. An exception is Christopher Baker, "Frost's 'After Apple-Picking' as Hypnagogic Vision."

6. In the original: "Dans le champ du rêve, au contraire, ce qui caractèrise les images, c'est que ça montre." Lacan, *Les Quatre Concepts fondamenteaux de la psychanalyse,* vol. 4 of *Le Séminaire de Jacques Lacan* (Paris: Éditions du Seuil, 1973), 72.

7. "The novel is the sole genre that continues to develop, that is as yet uncompleted" (Bakhtin 3).

8. There is an echo of Lane's concerns—as there is an echo of his title—in David Perkins's "Romantic Reading as Revery." Emphasizing the historicity of reading practices, Perkins analyzes the Romantic tendency to describe reading as an evocation of loosely associated thoughts accompanying the text that stimulates them. There is certainly a relationship between reverie and hypnagogia; for instance, Gaston Bachelard suggests that reverie, like hypnagogia, takes place on the edge of somnolence and can easily fall into actual dream (10). But there are also differences: reverie's mental images, half dissolved in thought and personal association, must be distinguished from the sharply focused and apparently impersonal images that flood hypnagogia's visual field.

9. Among Benjamin's later notes is one that resonates provocatively with Blanchot's theories: "Every image is a sleep in itself" (*On Hashish* 98). The link Benjamin makes between these images and the unconscious is also made by Freud, as he describes the state into which the analysand is to be brought: "What is in question, evidently, is the establishment of a psychical state which, in its distribution of psychical energy (that is, of mobile attention) bears some analogy to the state before falling asleep—and no doubt also to hypnosis. As we fall asleep, 'involuntary ideas' emerge, owing to the relaxation of a certain deliberate (and no doubt also critical) activity which we allow to influence the course of our ideas while we are awake. . . . As the involuntary ideas emerge they change into visual and acoustic images" (*Interpretation of Dreams* 4:134).

10. Studies in the ways that imaginative visualizing functions in reading include Christopher Collins, *The Poetics of the Mind's Eye;* Ellen Esrock, *The Reader's Eye;* Elaine Scarry, *Dreaming by the Book;* and my own *Fantasm and Fiction.*

11. As a comparison with the original text will show, Scarry fails to complete the sentence beginning "An empty egg-basket was slung upon his arm," which continues "the nap of his hat was ruffled, a patch being quite worn away at its brim where his thumb came in taking it off" (Hardy 13). Why she should silently omit this portion is puzzling, since it vividly contributes to her point about how texts direct a reader's attention.

12. I use the best-known, and probably best, translation of Wittgenstein's maxim "Wenn die Menschen nicht manchmal Dummheiten machten, geschähe überhaupt nichts Gescheites," from *Culture and Value* (57).

13. For the Romantics this wandering was a valued aspect of reading. According to Francis Jeffrey, a reader "is often indebted to the author for little more than an impulse, or the key-note of a melody which his fancy makes out for himself." Jeffrey is quoted by David Perkins in "Romantic Reading as Revery" (186), in which he discusses an associative mode of reading that was widely accepted by the Romantics and has since been denigrated and forgotten. The recent rise of cognitive psychology, among other developments, suggests a renewed attention to processes that might previously have been dismissed as irrelevant to reading. See Mary Thomas Crane and Alan Richardson, "Literary Studies and Cognitive Science"; and Andrew Elfenbein, "Cognitive Science and the History of Reading."

14. Blanchot shares Sarraute's cynicism about the inadequacy of the modernist interior monologue, as well as her sense of what is hidden beneath it: "Interior monologue is a coarse imitation, and one that imitates only the apparent traits of the uninterrupted and incessant flow of unspeaking speech. Let us recall that the strength of this speech is its weakness; it is not heard, which is why we don't stop hearing it; it is as close as possible to silence, which is why it destroys silence completely. Finally, interior monologue has a center, the 'I' that brings everything back to itself, while that other speech has no center; it is essentially wandering and always outside" (*The Book to Come* 223).

15. Fioretos's project is akin to William James's: "It is, in short, the reinstatement of the vague to its proper place in our mental life which I am so anxious to press on the attention" (1:254).

16. All quotations from *Agatha* are taken from this translation.

17. In "Extracts from the Log-Book of Monsieur Teste," Valéry has his protagonist pray to a god who is also the night, asking that he might attain the supreme thought—only to change his mind: "Grant, O Darkness—grant the supreme thought. . . . But any generally ordinary thought may be the 'supreme thought.' If it were otherwise, if there were one thought *supreme in itself* and *of itself*, we could discover it by reflection or by chance; and once it was found, we should have to die. That would mean being able to die of a particular thought, merely because there was none to follow" (*Monsieur Teste* 35). *Agatha* was at one point conceived of as the night side of *La Soiree avec Monsieur Teste*, the "*interior* of Teste's night" (*Poems in the Rough* 318).

18. See the section assembled as "Dream" in Valéry's *Cahiers/Notebooks*

(3:404–573). Aside from cumulatively yielding a remarkable, and remarkably overlooked, theory of the nature of dream, Valéry's notebook entries offer a fascinating glimpse of the way that a mind thinks through a difficult problem: trying on ideas, dropping them only to return to them, adopting contradictory stances, saying the same thing innumerable times in different words, extending the theories bit by bit without ever coming to a complete closure.

2. SLEEPLESS

1. On the effects and implications of the *Ganzfeld,* see Brian Massumi, "Chaos in the 'Total Field' of Vision."

2. "Poets Never Sleep," a dissertation by Angelica B. Ushatova focusing on Russian and German poetry about insomnia, supports this contention with a partial list of insomniac authors: William Shakespeare, Edward Young, Charles Dickens, Emily Brontë, Lewis Carroll, Charles Baudelaire, Marcel Proust, Gustave Flaubert, Stendhal, Fyodor Dostoyevsky, F. Scott Fitzgerald, Ernest Hemingway, Elizabeth Bishop, Stéphane Mallarmé, André Gide, Anton Chekhov, Franz Kafka, Henry Miller, Jorge Luis Borges, and Vladimir Nabokov. She follows this with a list of sleepless poets: Homer, Sappho, Martin Opitz, William Wordsworth, Annette von Droste-Hülshoff, Aleksandr Pushkin, Fyodor Tyutchev, Walt Whitman, D. H. Lawrence, Bertolt Brecht, Rainer Maria Rilke, Marina Tsvetayeva, Anna Akhmatova, Paul Celan (3–4). As Ushatova admits, there are many more.

3. Examples of such anthologies are *Night Walks,* edited by Joyce Carol Oates; *Hello Midnight,* edited by Deborah Bishop and David Levy; and Lisa Russ Spaar's *Acquainted with the Night.* There is virtually no end to the literary treatments of this subject—but I am more concerned here with making a theoretical argument than in surveying the various ways that insomnia is represented in literature.

4. In his diary entry for September 23, 1912, recording his intense overnight composition of "The Judgment," Kafka admits to "thoughts of Freud, of course." And speaking of the applicability of Freudianism to Kafka's works on the whole, Max Brod wrote that his friend "was thoroughly familiar with these theories," even if "he never regarded them as anything more than a very approximate, rough picture of things" (21–22).

5. I have substituted Mark Harmon's translation for the Muir translation that Cohn uses.

6. An interesting example of this is given in a letter Tennyson wrote in 1874 to the American mystic and writer Benjamin Paul Flood. He speaks of

a "waking trance" that he has found himself able to generate since boyhood; this comes about, he says, "through repeating my own name to myself silently, till all at once as it were out of the intensity of the consciousness of individuality the individuality itself seemed to dissolve and fade away into boundless being" (*Major Works* 520).

3. LEAVING SLEEP

1. Compare Levinas's image with Kafka's: "I think of those nights at the end of which I was raised out of sleep and awoke as though I had been folded in a nut" (*Diaries* 40).

2. Additional translation mine from the German given by Joel Morris.

3. Blanchot here passes by the narrative element that often plays an important role in dream, perhaps because it is not the narrative dynamic but the associative one that gives dreams their distinctive and disconcerting character. For Valéry, in fact, the narratives that are the only part of our dream life that we retain are actively misleading: "Recording this dream, I write it like a story, *summing it up,* giving the resumé of a story as it is remembered. That's the fundamental mistake that people make when recording dreams. Unfortunately there is no other way to do it. To arrive at the synthesis of a dream you would have to describe its 'atomic' constituents. Because a story—, *that you remember,* is only a secondary artefact based on a primary state that is not chronological, NOT TO BE SUMMED UP, cannot be *integrated*" (*Cahiers* 3:486). The complex relation of dreams to narrative is not within the scope of this book; it is the central concern of another book, *Dreaming and Storytelling* by Bert O. States.

4. Nietzsche anticipates Lacan's more developed argument. Writing in *Twilight of the Idols* of how external sensations registered in dreams are assigned causes within the dream world, he concludes, "We do just the same thing, in fact, when we are awake" (60). My thanks to Rob Switzer for this reference.

5. Compare Freud on the limits of his own method: "There is no possibility of *explaining* dreams as a psychical process, since to explain a thing means to trace it back to something already known" (*Interpretation of Dreams* 549).

4. SLEEPWAKING

1. Xiaoqiang Han, "Interpreting the Butterfly Dream," 3.

2. See Thomas Nagel, "What Is It Like To Be a Bat?" The essay by Jung H. Lee to which Han is responding is titled "What Is It Like To Be a Butterfly? A Philosophical Interpretation of Zhuangzi's Butterfly Dream."

3. This is Hans-Georg Möller's main point in "Zhuangzi's 'Dream of the Butterfly.'"

4. Richard E. Aquila footnotes this as follows: "It is not perfectly clear what text Schopenhauer has in mind here, but probably A224-6/B272-4." Jeremy Greenway has pointed out to me that a more likely source is A492/B520 in the *Critique of Pure Reason*. The passage, in Norman Kemp Smith's translation, reads: "The empirical truth of appearances in space and time is . . . adequately distinguished from dreams, if both dreams and genuine appearances cohere truly and completely in one experience, in accordance with empirical laws. . . . For everything is real which stands in connection with a perception in accordance with the laws of empirical advance. They are therefore real if they stand in an empirical connection with my actual consciousness, although they are not for that reason real in themselves, that is, outside this advance of experience" (440–41).

5. Studies of Pessoa's influence include Irene Ramalho Santos's *Atlantic Poets* and George Monteiro's *The Presence of Pessoa*.

6. Tabucchi's critical writings on Pessoa have been collected in *Un baule pieno di gente*.

7. In 2004 Tabucchi translated *The Book of Disquiet* into Italian.

8. What Sollers says of Mallarmé in "Literature and Totality" may also be applied to him: that he belongs to what Blanchot calls "the impetuous, insistent literature that no longer tolerates distinctions between genres and seeks to burst their limits" (65).

9. "Le mot *drame* est ici employé dans son sense le plus ancien, non pas celui d' 'action'—encore moins celui d'intrigue psychologique—mais plutôt celui d' 'histoire,' d' 'événement.'" English translation by Philip Beitchman. Beitchman cites a pertinent passage in "Literature and Totality," an essay first delivered as a lecture for Roland Barthes's seminar in 1965, the year in which *Drame* was published: "WE MUST THEREFORE REALIZE THE POSSIBILITY OF THE TEXT AS THEATRE ALONG WITH THAT OF THE THEATRE AND OF LIFE AS TEXT if we want to take our place within the writing that defines us" (82). The theater in Sollers's novel, as will become evident, is less that of the text itself than it is that of the elusive play in the mind while the text is evolving.

10. All English quotations are from the translation by Bruce Benderson and Ursule Molinaro, which I have sometimes modified slightly.

11. Blanchot's "ray" is probably a reference to Husserl's "ray of regard" (*Ideas* 52, 222), an "attentive, seizing" activity (51) characteristic of the waking state. If Blanchot now makes this the ray of a *star*, it is probably because a star's ray is, after all, the merest twinkle in a sea of night.

12. Personal communication, August 15, 2010.

13. Personal communication, August 20, 2010.

14. For a related treatment of the book's paradoxes of appearance/disappearance, see my "*Agrippa*, or, The Apocalyptic Book."

BIBLIOGRAPHY

Agamben, Giorgio. *The Coming Community*. Translated by Michael Hardt. Minneapolis: University of Minnesota Press, 2007.

Alvarez, A. *Night: An Exploration of Night Life, Night Language, Sleep, and Dream*. New York: Vintage Books, 1996.

Ashbery, John. "Craft Interview with John Ashbery." Conducted by Janet Bloom and Robert Losada. *New York Quarterly*, no. 9 (Winter 1972): 11–33.

———. "Interview with John Ashbery." Conducted by John Koethe. *SubStance* 37–38 (1983): 178–86.

———. Interview with John Ashbery conducted by Peter Stitt. In *Poets at Work: The "Paris Review" Interviews*, edited by George Plimpton, 389–412. New York: Viking Press, 1989.

———. "John Ashbery." Interview conducted by Sue Gangel. In *American Poetry Observed: Poets on Their Work*, edited by Joe David Bellamy, 9–20. Urbana: University of Illinois Press, 1984.

———. "Notes about the Process: An Interview with John Ashbery." Conducted by Rodrigo Garcia Lopes. *Hayden's Ferry Review* 12 (Spring/Summer 1993): 27–33.

———. "A Tone Poem." In *As We Know*. New York: Viking Press, 1979.

Bachelard, Gaston. *The Poetics of Reverie: Childhood, Language, and the Cosmos*. Translated by Daniel Russell. Boston: Beacon Press, 1969.

Baker, Christopher. "Frost's 'After Apple-Picking' as Hypnagogic Vision." *Robert Frost Review* (Fall 1994): 28–32.

Bakhtin, Mikhail. "Epic and Novel." In *The Dialogic Imagination: Four Essays*. Translated by Caryl Emerson and Michael Holquist, 3–40. Austin: University of Texas Press, 1981.

Barnes, Djuna. *Nightwood*. Edited by Cheryl J. Plumb. New York: Dalkey Archive Press, 1995.

Barthes, Roland. "Event, Poem, Novel." In Philippe Sollers, *Event*. Translated by Bruce Benderson and Ursule Molinaro, 85–104. New York: Red Dust, 1986.

————. *The Pleasure of the Text*. Translated by Richard Miller. New York: Hill & Wang, 1975.

————. "The Rustle of Language." In *The Rustle of Language*. Translated by Richard Howard, 76–79. New York: Hill & Wang, 1986.

Beitchman, Philip. *I Am a Process with No Subject*. Gainesville: University of Florida Press, 1988.

Bellemin-Noël, Jean. "Psychoanalytic Reading and the Avant-texte." In *Genetic Criticism: Texts and Avant-textes*, edited by Jed Deppman, Daniel Ferrer, and Michael Groden, 28–35. Philadelphia: University of Pennsylvania Press, 2004.

Benjamin, Walter. "Breakfast Room." In *Walter Benjamin: Selected Writings*. Vol. 1 (1913–26), edited by Marcus Bullock and Michael W. Jennings, 444–45. Cambridge, Mass.: Belknap Press, 1996.

————. *On Hashish*. Translated by Howard Eiland et al. Cambridge, Mass.: Belknap Press, 2006.

————. "On the Image of Proust." In *Selected Writings*. Vol. 2, pt. 1 (1927–30). Translated by Rodney Livingstone et al., 237–47. Cambridge, Mass.: Belknap Press, 1999.

————. "The Storyteller." In *Illuminations*, 83–109. New York: Schocken, 1969.

Bishop, Deborah, and David Levy, eds. *Hello Midnight: An Insomniac's Literary Bedside Companion*. New York: Simon & Schuster, 2001.

Blanchot, Maurice. *The Book to Come*. Translated by Charlotte Mandell. Stanford, Calif.: Stanford University Press, 2003.

————. "Dreaming, Writing." In Michel Leiris, *Nights as Day, Days as Night*. Translated by Richard Sieburth, xix–xxviii. Hygiene, Colo.: Eridanos Press, 1987.

————. *Friendship*. Translated by Elizabeth Rottenberg. Stanford, Calif.: Stanford University Press, 1997.

————. *The Infinite Conversation*. Translated by Susan Hanson. Minneapolis: University of Minnesota Press, 1993.

————. *The Space of Literature*. Translated by Ann Smock. Lincoln: University of Nebraska Press, 1989.

————. *The Writing of the Disaster.* Translated by Ann Smock. Lincoln: University of Nebraska Press, 1995.

Borges, Jorge Luis. *Brodie's Report* [1970]. Translated by Andrew Hurley. New York: Penguin, 2005.

Botz-Bornstein, Thorsten. "Khôra or Idyll? The Space of the Dream." *Philosophical Forum* 33, no. 2 (Summer 2002): 173–94.

Breton, André. *Communicating Vessels.* Translated by Mary Ann Caws and Geoffrey T. Harris. Lincoln: University of Nebraska Press, 1990.

————. *What Is Surrealism? Selected Writings.* Edited by Franklin Rosemont. Translated by John Ashbery et al. London: Pluto Press, 1978.

Broch, Hermann. *The Sleepwalkers.* Translated by Willa Muir and Edwin Muir. New York: Pantheon, 1947.

Brod, Max. "Kafka: Father and Son." *Partisan Review* 4 (May 1938): 19–29.

Butler, Blake. *Nothing: A Portrait of Insomnia.* New York: HarperPerennial, 2011.

Carson, Anne. "Every Exit Is an Entrance (A Praise of Sleep)." *Prairiefire* 25, no. 3 (Autumn 2004): 6–21.

Céline, Louis-Ferdinand. *Death on the Installment Plan.* Translated by Ralph Manheim. New York: New Directions, 1971.

Chaucer, Geoffrey. "Book of the Duchess." In *The Complete Poetry and Prose of Geoffrey Chaucer,* edited by John H. Fisher, 544–62. Toronto: Holt, Rinehart & Winston, 1977.

Cioran, E. M. *A Short History of Decay.* Translated by Richard Howard. New York: Arcade, 1975.

————. *The Trouble with Being Born.* Translated by Richard Howard. Chicago: Quadrangle, 1976.

Cohn, Dorrit. "Castles and Anti-castles, or Kafka and Robbe-Grillet." *Novel* 5, no. 1 (Fall 1971): 19–31.

Coleridge, Samuel Taylor. *The Complete Poems.* Edited by William Keach. New York: Penguin, 1997.

Collins, Christopher. *The Poetics of the Mind's Eye: Literature and the Psychology of Imagination.* Philadelphia: University of Pennsylvania Press, 1991.

Conrad, Joseph. *The Nigger of the Narcissus.* New York: Doubleday, 1959.

Crane, Mary Thomas, and Alan Richardson. "Literary Studies and Cognitive Science: Toward a New Interdisciplinarity." *Mosaic* 32, no. 2 (1999): 123–40.

Davis, Kevin K. "Hypnogony: The Sleep of Philosophy—An Art of Sleep." M.A. thesis, University of Western Ontario, Centre for the Study of Theory and Criticism, 2000.

De Chirico, Giorgio. *Hebdomeros.* Translated by John Ashbery et al. Cambridge: Exact Change, 1992.

Dennett, Daniel. "Are Dreams Experiences?" *Philosophical Review* 85, no. 2 (April 1976): 151–71.

———. *Consciousness Explained.* Boston: Little, Brown, 1991.

Descartes, René. *The Philosophical Writings of Descartes.* Vol. 2. Translated by John Cottingham, Robert Stoothoff, and Dugald Murdoch. Cambridge: Cambridge University Press, 1984.

Dickinson, Emily. *The Complete Poems of Emily Dickinson.* Edited by Thomas H. Johnson. Boston: Little, Brown, 1961.

Elfenbein, Andrew. "Cognitive Science and the History of Reading." *PMLA* 121, no. 2 (2006): 484–502.

Ellmann, Richard. *James Joyce.* New York: Oxford University Press, 1959.

Esrock, Ellen. *The Reader's Eye: Visual Imaging as Reader Response.* Baltimore: Johns Hopkins University Press, 1994.

Evenson, Brian. "Taking Things for Granted." *Symploke* 14, nos. 1–2 (2006): 323–27.

Farbman, Herschel. *The Other Night: Dreaming, Writing, and Restlessness in Twentieth-Century Literature.* New York: Fordham University Press, 2008.

Federman, Raymond. "What Are Experimental Novels and Why Are There So Many Left Unread?" *Genre: Forms of Discourse and Culture* 14, no. 1 (Spring 1981): 23–31.

Fioretos, Aris. *The Gray Book.* Stanford, Calif.: University of Stanford Press, 1999.

Foucault, Michel. "Language to Infinity." In *Language, Counter-memory, Practice: Selected Essays and Interviews.* Edited and translated by Donald F. Bouchard, 53–67. Ithaca, N.Y.: Cornell University Press, 1977.

Freud, Sigmund. *Beyond the Pleasure Principle* [1920]. In *The Standard Edition of the Complete Psychological Works of Sigmund Freud.* Vol. 18. Translated by James Strachey. London: Hogarth Press, 1975.

———. *The Interpretation of Dreams.* Vols. 4–5 of *The Standard Edition of the Complete Psychological Works of Sigmund Freud.* Translated by James Strachey. London: Hogarth Press, 1975.

———. "Mourning and Melancholia." Translated by James Strachey. In *On Metapsychology.* Vol. 2 of *The Penguin Freud Library,* 247–67. New York: Penguin, 1984.

Frost, Robert. "After Apple-Picking." In *The Poetry of Robert Frost*. Edited by Edward Connery Lathem, 68–69. New York: Holt, Rinehart & Winston, 1969.

Garland, Alex. *The Coma*. New York: Riverhead, 2004.

Gernsbacher, Morton Ann, and Michael P. Kaschak. "Neuroimaging Studies of Language Production and Comprehension." *Annual Review of Psychology* 54 (2003): 91–114.

Gerrig, Richard J. *Experiencing Narrative Worlds: On the Psychological Activities of Reading*. New Haven, Conn.: Yale University Press, 1993.

Han, Xiaoqiang. "Interpreting the Butterfly Dream." *Asian Philosophy* 19, no. 1 (March 2009): 1–9.

Hardy, Thomas. *Tess of the d'Urbervilles*. Edited by Juliet Grindle and Simon Gatrell. Oxford: Clarendon Press, 1983.

Hegel, G. W. F. *Hegel's Philosophy of Mind*. Translated by William Wallace and A. V. Miller. Oxford: Oxford University Press, 1971.

Heidegger, Martin. *Zollikon Seminars: Protocols–Conversations–Letters*. Edited by Medard Boss. Translated by Franz Mayr and Richard Askay. Evanston, Ill.: Northwestern University Press, 2001.

Hunt, Laird. *Ray of the Star*. Minneapolis: Coffee House Press, 2009.

Husserl, Edmund. *Ideas Pertaining to a Pure Phenomenology and to a Phenomenological Philosophy*, book 1. Translated by F. Kersten. The Hague: Martinus Nijhoff, 1983.

Irwin, Robert. *The Arabian Nightmare*. Woodstock, N.Y.: Overlook Press, 2002.

Iser, Wolfgang. *The Act of Reading: A Theory of Aesthetic Response*. Baltimore: Johns Hopkins University Press, 1978.

James, William. *Principles of Psychology*. 2 vols. New York: Dover, 1950.

Janouch, Gustav. *Conversations with Kafka*. Translated by Goronwy Rees. New York: New Directions, 1971.

Johnson, Greg. "'On the Edge of an Abyss': The Writer as Insomniac." *Virginia Quarterly Review* 66, no. 4 (1990): 643–55.

Joyce, James. *Finnegans Wake*. New York: Penguin, 1999.

Kafka, Franz. *The Castle*. Translated by Mark Harmon. New York: Schocken, 1998.

———. *The Complete Stories*. Edited by Nahum N. Glatzer. New York: Schocken, 1971.

———. *The Diaries of Franz Kafka, 1910–1923*. Edited by Max Brod. Translated by Joseph Kresh et al. New York: Schocken, 1988.

———. *Letters to Felice*. Translated by James Stern and Elisabeth Duckworth. New York: Schocken, 1973.

————. *The Trial.* Translated by Edwin Muir and Wilma Muir. New York: Schocken, 1995.

Kant, Immanuel. *Critique of Pure Reason.* Translated by Norman Kemp Smith. London: Macmillan, 1958.

King, Stephen. "Harvey's Dream." In *Just After Sunset,* 85–94. New York: Charles Scribner's Sons, 2008.

Kiš, Danilo. *Garden, Ashes.* Translated by William J. Hannacher. New York: Harcourt Brace Jovanovich, 1975.

Knapp, Bettina. *French Novelists Speak Out.* Troy, N.Y.: Whitston, 1976.

Kunin, Aaron. *The Mandarin.* Albany, N.Y.: Fence Books, 2008.

Kurijaka, Susan Katherine Hopkins. "'Waking Dream': Hawthorne's Hypnagogic Image of the Imagination." Ph.D. diss., University of North Carolina, Chapel Hill, 1992.

Lacan, Jacques. *The Four Fundamental Concepts of Psychoanalysis.* Book 11 of *The Seminar of Jacques Lacan.* Edited by Jacques-Alain Miller. Translated by Alan Sheridan. New York: W. W. Norton, 1998.

————. "Improvisation: Désir de mort, rêve et réveil." Response to Catherine Millot. *L'Ane* 198, no. 3 (Autumn 1981): 3. http://www.valas.fr/Jacques -Lacan-Desir-de-mort-reve-et-reveil,053.

Lane, Jeremy. "Falling Asleep in the *Wake*: Reading as Hypnagogic Experience." In *Re:Joyce: Text, Culture, Politics,* edited by John Brannigan, Geoff Ward, and Julian Wolfreys, 163–81. New York: Palgrave Macmillan, 1998.

Lawrence, Karen. *The Odyssey of Style in "Ulysses."* Princeton, N.J.: Princeton University Press, 1981.

Lee, Jung H. "What Is It Like To Be a Butterfly? A Philosophical Interpretation of Zhuangzi's Butterfly Dream." *Asian Philosophy* 17, no. 2 (July 2007): 185–202.

Leiris, Michel. *Nights as Day, Days as Night.* Translated by Richard Sieburth. Hygiene, Colo.: Eridanos Press, 1987.

Lerner, Ben. "Aaron Kunin in Conversation with Ben Lerner." Jacket Magazine, 2009. http://jacketmagazine.com/37/iv-kunin-ivb-lerner.shtml.

Levinas, Emmanuel. *Existence and Existents.* Translated by Alphonso Lingis. Pittsburgh: Dusquene University Press, 2001.

Linschoten, Jan, "On Falling Asleep." In *Phenomenological Psychology: The Dutch School,* edited by Joseph J. Kockelmans, 149–94. Dordrecht: Martinus Nijhoff, 1987.

Llinas, R. R., and D. Paré. "Of Dreaming and Wakefulness." *Neuroscience* 44, no. 3 (1991): 521–35.

Mallarmé, Stéphane. "Variations sur un sujet." In *Oeuvres Complètes,* edited by Henri Mondor and G. Jean-Aubry, 355–68. Paris: Gallimard [Bibliothèque de la Pleiade], 1945.

Marcus, Ben. "Why Experimental Fiction Threatens To Destroy Publishing, Jonathan Franzen, and Life as We Know It: A Correction." *Harper's Magazine,* October 2005, 39–52.

Massumi, Brian. "Chaos in the 'Total Field' of Vision. " In *Parables for the Virtual: Movement, Affect, Sensation,* 144–61. Durham, N.C.: Duke University Press, 2002.

Mavromatis, Andreas. *Hypnagogia: The Unique State of Consciousness between Wakefulness and Sleep.* London: Routledge, 1991.

Merleau-Ponty, Maurice. *Institution and Passivity: Course Notes from the Collège de France (1954–1955).* Translated by Leonard Lawlor and Heath Massey. Evanston, Ill.: Northwestern University Press, 2010.

———. *Phenomenology of Perception.* Translated by Colin Smith. London: Routledge, 2001.

Michels, Agnes Kirsopp. "The *Insomnium* of Aeneas." *Classical Quarterly* 31, no. 1 (1981): 140–46.

Miura, Nobutaka. "Sommeil et réveil chez Valéry: D'Agathe à La Jeune Parque." *Études de Langue et Litterature Françaises* 38 (1981): 72–110.

Möller, Hans-Georg. "Zhuangzi's 'Dream of the Butterfly': A Daoist Interpretation." *Philosophy East and West* 49, no. 4 (October 1999): 439–50.

Monteiro, George. *The Presence of Pessoa: English, American, and Southern African Literary Responses.* Lexington: University Press of Kentucky, 1998.

Morris, Joel. "Josef K's (A + x) Problem: Kafka on the Moment of Awakening." *German Quarterly* 82, no. 4 (Fall 2009): 469–82.

Nabokov, Vladimir. *Pale Fire.* New York: Vintage Books, 1989.

———. *Speak, Memory: An Autobiography Revisited.* New York: G. P. Putnam's Sons, 1966.

Nagel, Thomas. "What Is It Like To Be a Bat?" *Philosophical Review* 83 (1974): 435–50.

Nancy, Jean-Luc. *The Fall of Sleep.* Translated by Charlotte Mandell. New York: Fordham University Press, 2009.

———. "Identity and Trembling." In *The Birth to Presence.* Translated by Brian Holmes, 9–35. Stanford, Calif.: Stanford University Press, 1993.

Nell, Victor. *Lost in a Book: The Psychology of Reading for Pleasure.* New Haven, Conn.: Yale University Press, 1988.

Nesbitt, Lois Ellen. "Critical Insomnia: Reading and Rereading Joyce, Proust, and Beckett." Ph.D. diss., Princeton University, 1988.

Nietzsche, Friedrich. *Beyond Good and Evil.* Translated by Marion Faber. Oxford: Oxford University Press, 1998.

———. *Daybreak: Thoughts on the Prejudices of Morality*. Translated by R. J. Hollingdale. Cambridge: Cambridge University Press, 1997.

———. *Twilight of the Idols; or, How To Philosophize with a Hammer*. Translated by Duncan Large. Oxford: Oxford University Press, 1998.

Oates, Joyce Carol, ed. *Night Walks: A Bedside Companion*. Princeton, N.J.: Ontario Review Press, 1982.

Oswald, Ian. *Sleeping and Waking: Physiology and Psychology*. Amsterdam: Elsevier, 1962.

Perkins, David. "Romantic Reading as Revery." *European Romantic Review* 4, no. 2 (1994): 183–99.

Pessoa, Fernando. *The Book of Disquiet*. Translated by Alfred MacAdam. Cambridge: Exact Change, 1998.

Plato. *Theaetetus*. Translated by Benjamin Jowett. Rockville, Md.: Serenity, 2009.

Poe, Edgar Allan. "Marginalia 150" [1846]. In *The Brevities: "Pinakidia," "Marginalia," "Fifty Suggestions," and Other Works*. Vol. 2 of *Collected Writings of Edgar Allan Poe*, edited by Burton R. Pollin, 257–59. New York: Gordian Press, 1985.

Poulet, Georges. "Criticism and the Experience of Interiority." In *Reader-Response Criticism: From Formalism to Post-structuralism*, edited by Jane P. Tompkins, 41–49. Baltimore: Johns Hopkins University Press, 1980.

Proust, Marcel. *The Way by Swann's*. Vol. 1 of *In Search of Lost Time*. Translated by Lydia Davis. London: Penguin Classics, 2003.

Queneau, Raymond. *The Blue Flowers*. Translated by Barbara Wright. New York: New Directions, 1985.

———. *Une Histoire modéle*. Paris: Gallimard, 1966.

———. *Stories and Remarks*. Translated by Marc Lowenthal. Lincoln: University of Nebraska Press, 2000.

Regier, Willis G. "Cioran's Insomnia." *MLN* 119 (2004): 994–1012.

Santos, Irene Ramalho. *Atlantic Poets: Fernando Pessoa's Turn in Anglo-American Modernism*. Hanover, N.H.: University Press of New England, 2003.

Sarraute, Nathalie. "Conversation and Sub-conversation." In *The Age of Suspicion: Essays on the Novel*. Translated by Maria Jolas, 77–117. New York: George Braziller, 1963.

Sartre, Jean-Paul. *The Psychology of Imagination*. Translated by publisher. New York: Philosophical Library, 1948.

Scarry, Elaine. *Dreaming by the Book*. New York: Farrar, Straus and Giroux, 1999.

Schopenhauer, Arthur. *The World as Will and Presentation.* Vol. 1. Translated by Richard E. Aquila. Toronto: Pearson, 2008.

Schwenger, Peter. *"Agrippa,* or, The Apocalyptic Book." In *Flame Wars: The Discourse of Cyberculture,* edited by Mark Dery, 61–70. Durham, N.C.: Duke University Press, 1994.

———. *Fantasm and Fiction: On Textual Envisioning.* Stanford, Calif.: Stanford University Press, 1991.

———. "Writing Hypnagogia." *Critical Inquiry* 34, no. 3 (Spring 2008): 423–39.

Sollers, Philippe. *Drame: Roman.* Paris: Éditions du Seuil, 1965.

———. *Event.* Translated by Bruce Benderson and Ursule Molinaro. New York: Red Dust, 1986.

———. "Literature and Totality." In *Writing and the Experience of Limits.* Translated by Philip Barnard and David Hayman, 63–85. New York: Columbia University Press, 1983.

———. *Logiques.* Paris: Éditions du Seuil, 1968.

———. "The Novel and the Experience of Limits." In *Writing and the Experience of Limits.* Translated by Philip Barnard and David Hayman, 185–208. New York: Columbia University Press, 1983.

Spaar, Lisa Russ, ed. *Acquainted with the Night: Insomnia Poems.* New York: Columbia University Press, 1999.

States, Bert O. *Dreaming and Storytelling.* Ithaca, N.Y.: Cornell University Press, 1991.

———. *Seeing in the Dark: Reflections on Dreams and Dreaming.* New Haven, Conn.: Yale University Press, 1997.

Summers-Bremner, Eluned. *Insomnia: A Cultural History.* London: Reaktion, 2008.

Svevo, Italo. *Confessions of Zeno.* Translated by Beryl de Zoete. London: Secker & Warburg, 1962.

Switzer, Robert. "The Sleep of Reason: Phenomenology and Its Shadow." Unpublished paper.

Tabucchi, Antonio. *Un baule pieno di gente: Scritti su Fernando Pessoa.* Milan: Feltrinelli, 2000.

———. *The Edge of the Horizon.* Translated by Tim Parks. New York: New Directions, 1990.

———. *Indian Nocturne.* Translated by Tim Parks. London: Chatto & Windus, 1988.

———. "Postface: La Poétique de l'insomnie." In *Oeuvres de Fernando Pessoa III: Le Livre de l'Intranquillité de Bernardo Soares.* Translated by Françoise Lye, 263–69. Paris: Christian Bourgois, 1988.

————. *Requiem: A Hallucination.* Translated by Margaret Jull Costa. London: Harvill, 1994.

Tennyson, Alfred. *The Major Works.* Edited by Adam C. Roberts. Oxford: Oxford University Press, 2009.

Trentini, Nives. "Towards a Study of Dream in Antonio Tabucchi." Translated by John Gatt-Rutter. In *Antonio Tabucchi: A Collection of Essays,* edited by Bruno Ferraro and Nicole Prunster, 71–97. Bundoora, Victoria: Spunti e Ricerche, 1997.

Updike, John. "Tossing and Turning." In *Collected Poems, 1953–1993,* 109–10. New York: Alfred A. Knopf, 1993.

Ushatova, Angelica B. "Poets Never Sleep: Insomnia in Russian and German Poetry from the Seventeenth to the Twentieth Century." Ph.D. diss., Brandeis University, 2004.

Valéry, Paul. *Cahiers/Notebooks.* Vol. 3. Translated by Norma Rinsler, Paul Ryan, and Brian Stimpson. Frankfurt: Peter Lang, 2007.

————. *Monsieur Teste.* Vol. 6 of *The Collected Works of Paul Valéry.* Translated by Jackson Matthews. Princeton, N.J.: Princeton University Press, 1973.

———— *Poems in the Rough.* Vol. 2 of *The Collected Works of Paul Valéry.* Edited by Jackson Mathews. Translated by Hilary Corke. Princeton, N.J.: Princeton University Press, 1969.

Wackermann, Jirí, Peter Pütz, and Carsten Allefeld. "Ganzfeld-Induced Hallucinatory Experience, Its Phenomenology and Cerebral Electrophysiology." *Cortex* 44 (2008): 1364–78.

Wade, Nicholas J., and Josef Brozek. *Purkinje's Vision: The Dawning of Neuroscience.* Mahwah, N.J.: Lawrence Erlbaum, 2001.

Weller, Barry. "Pleasure and Self-Loss in Reading." *ADE Bulletin* 99 (Fall 1991): 8–12.

Wilbur, Richard. "Walking to Sleep." In *Walking to Sleep: New Poems and Translations,* 53–58. New York: Harcourt Brace World, 1969.

Winnard, Andrew. "'These Drowsy Approaches of Sleep': Christa Wolf and the Hypnagogic Dream." *New German Studies* 14, no. 3 (1987): 171–86.

Wittgenstein, Ludwig. *Culture and Value: A Selection from the Posthumous Remains.* Edited by George Henrik von Wright and Heikki Nyman. Translated by Peter Winch. Oxford: Blackwell, 1998.

Wojnarowicz, David. *Close to the Knives: A Memoir of Disintegration.* New York: Vintage Books, 1991.

Woolf, Virginia. "Modern Fiction." In *Collected Essays,* 2:103–10. London: Hogarth Press, 1966.

————. *The Waves.* New York: Harcourt Brace, 1959.

INDEX

PETER SCHWENGER is resident fellow at the Centre for the Study of Theory and Criticism, University of Western Ontario, and professor emeritus of English at Mount St. Vincent University. He is the author of several books, including *The Tears of Things: Melancholy and Physical Objects* (Minnesota, 2006) and *Fantasm and Fiction: On Textual Envisioning.*